WARRIOR WRITERS

Published by Iraq Veterans Against the War
Email: warriorwriters@ivaw.org
Website: www.ivaw.org

Printed by L. Brown and Sons Printing, Inc.
14-20 Jefferson Street
Barre, Vermont 05641

ISBN 978-0-9801665-0-7

Edited by Lovella Calica
Warrior Writers directors are Lovella Calica,
Drew Cameron, and Aaron Hughes
Designed and typeset by Becky Nasadowski

WARRIOR WRITERS
RE-MAKING SENSE

A COLLECTION OF ARTWORK BY
MEMBERS OF IRAQ VETERANS AGAINST THE WAR

This book is dedicated to Sammantha Owen-Ewing. In your silence, you speak.
December 7, 1986–November 26, 2007

THE WARRIOR WRITERS PROJECT

Lovella Calica, Editor

The Warrior Writers Project is a dynamic, organic journey that moves based on the creative processes, conversations, connections and needs of those involved. The Warrior Writers Project provides tools and space for community building, healing and redefinition for members of Iraq Veterans Against the War (IVAW). Through writing and artistic workshops that are based on experiences in the military and Iraq, IVAW members unbury experiences and connect with each other on a personal and artistic level. The writing and art from the workshops are compiled into books, performances and exhibits that provide a lens into the hearts of people who have a deep and intimate relationship with the Iraq war. Furthermore, the project gives the artists a sense of ownership over their stories and strength in their voice, perspective and power.

I have facilitated five writing workshops in various parts of the country for IVAW members and other veterans, military family members and allies. Each workshop is unique, though I follow similar formats and some pieces are staples. I use quotes from Maxine Hong Kingston, veterans and other inspirational people. We read and discuss writing—including poetry—by veterans. The workshops are given titles and themes that are created naturally through related texts, exercises and issues (conversations, ideas, hopes, etc.) that members are dealing with. The most important piece of this project is the workshops. This is a sacred time where members are quiet, reflective, empowered and connected. They are learning to heal themselves with the support of each other.

Writings that were created from the workshops are notated. Other pieces came from a call for submissions.

Workshops

(w1) Workshop 1 – Untitled
New York City, New York. February 10-11, 2007.

(w2) Workshop 2 – *Re-making Sense*
Burlington, Vermont. April 20-22, 2007.

(w3) Workshop 3 – *Intrusive Thoughts*
Chicago, Illinois. June 19, 2007.

(w4) Mini Workshop 4 – Untitled
St. Louis, Missouri (at Veterans for Peace Convention).
August 17, 2007.

(w5) Workshop 5 – *Convoy Ops*
Watertown, New York (near Fort Drum). October 13, 2007.

Workshop Assignments

□ Write a piece using one or more of the following phrases:
I am, Who survived, or *Forgive me.*

■ Write a letter from your current self to the person you will
be in ten years.

▣ React to a photo from your military service that tells the story
behind the image. Describe the things the picture cannot tell.

▫ Write your thoughts on coming home.

○ Write about a body part.

● Respond to a photo transfer.

Other

= Letters

► Photographs, transfers, and other artwork

CONTENTS

SECTION THREE

INTRODUCTION
Jan Barry

Waging war is the hard, harsh work of armies. Writing about that experience should also be hard and harsh. This point is memorably made in this collection of poetry, prose and art sponsored by Iraq Veterans Against the War. This writing is raw, edgy and meant to shock readers into feeling what it's like, for an instant, to be in a soldier's skin when war memories intrude into civilian life.

These explosive works flare out of the pages of a carefully crafted anthology of soldiers' unrelenting reexamination of what happened and why. The collection is full of intense insights that illuminate the big questions about the bitter wars in Asia and warfare in general—challenging the mythology of military veterans as stoic saviors of civil society's virtues and values.

It is hard to fit into a life where everyone around me has no understanding that I lived my life for a year in a place where every decision I made either killed someone, or saved someone. I hope that in time we as veterans will find a way to bring our experience from war into society so our children will know the truth: war makes monsters of us all," former infantryman Mark "Gordy" Lachance wrote in an essay published in an earlier, chapbook version titled *Warrior Writers: Move, Shoot and Communicate.*

"Never again must we fall into the belief that a 'band of brothers' is something only achievable while making war on others … We must see a brotherhood for what it truly is, an ultimate expression of love, and we must remember it is not something we can enforce and foster with a rifle," added a fellow infantryman, Paul Abernathy.

This theme was extended even further to the people at the other end of American guns in this latest, larger collection, such as in the poem "You Are Not My Enemy," by former artilleryman Drew Cameron:

You are not my enemy
we will change this,
with you.

In addition to this anthology and the inaugural chapbook, similarly stark writings, photos and artwork by War on Terror veterans has been displayed at the National Vietnam Veterans Art Museum in Chicago. "When I got back from the war I did not want to tell any-one anything but instead just to reflect and think," Aaron Hughes, one of the organizers of the art show in Chicago and a contributor to Warrior Writers, wrote on his web site, www.aarhughes.org/blog. Now he and other vets of Iraq and Afghanistan are working hard through harsh recollections to find their own voices and visions.

Jan Barry is the coeditor of *Winning Hearts & Minds: War Poems by Vietnam Veterans* and *Demilitarized Zones: Veterans After Vietnam*

EDITOR'S NOTES

Lovella Calica

"THE DEEPER THAT SORROW CARVES INTO YOUR BEING,
THE MORE JOY YOU CAN CONTAIN."

Khalil Gibran

First, I give thanks to all the Warrior Writers who have trusted me with their hearts, time and stories. It is a great honor to be involved in this project.

The works in this collection come from the need to be honest and real, to express the most painful and complex emotions related to military experiences, specifically those connected to the occupation of Iraq. There is a deep necessity to create when so much has been shattered and stolen—a profound sense of hope comes from the ability to rebuild.

Workshops begin by discussing how we can use writing as a tool for expressing ourselves, dealing with emotions, understanding consequences and relating to each other. Although it is often challenging and exhausting for veterans to write, relive events, reflect and try to describe their feelings, this process helps lighten the weight of their memories and thoughts. Then the veterans read their writing aloud. For many, it is the first time they have ever spoken honestly about their experiences and feelings to others. It is incredibly empowering for them to read what they have written out loud, to give voice to the silence that weighs so heavily on them. It is a very delicate place to be. Processing and creating art together is critical. In a community of people that understand, do not judge and can offer genuine support, there is space to heal and grow. As veterans, they have similar experiences, and it is imperative to make connections with each other to avoid isolation. The atmosphere we create is sacred, and they acknowledge its value.

The veterans are learning how to move out of the past into the future, using their emotions and experiences to build the rest of their lives. The Warrior Writers Project gives IVAW members a space to create, express themselves and be proud. They are confident in what they are creating and can see them-selves as artists or writers, not only veterans. They are redefining themselves and using their history to heal themselves and others. The way writing and expression moves them is powerful and inspiring. I am honored to create spaces that offer hope and assurance that we can survive and that we can transform ourselves and our lives.

I am always a survivor
I AM ALWAYS A SURVIVOR
it is in my blood, my bones, my mouth
in my skin, my hair, my breath
in my voice, my eyes, my hands
it is in my hands as I use these once wound fingers to process, to
think, to grow, to create, to leave pain behind
to shape it into something strong, to give me power, hope, healing
I am re-making my hands, I am defining their role in my life
they will not be his tool for power or pleasure or pain
but MY TOOLS for strength, hope and Love
for creation, for nurturing, for Life
we are searching for truth
discovering truth
questioning truth
creating truth
becoming truth
we are sharing

December, 2007
Agoo, La Union, Philippines

IT BEGINS
WE SHALL BUILD ON THE LITERARY TRADITION
OF VETERANS WHO OPEN THAT
CAPSULE OF BURDEN
SWALLOWED WHOLE, ABSORBED FULLY
CERTAIN MEMORIES WILL COME
TO BEAR ON THE CONSCIOUSNESS
OF US ALL
RE-MAKING SENSE

Drew Cameron

WE HAD CHANGED THEIR LANGUAGE
JUST BY OUR IGNORANCE.

Paul Abernathy

GO BACK TO WORK ON MONDAY
AND PUT ON THE UNIFORM AND PLAY THE GAME.

Eli Wright

Monday, March 17, 2003
Subject: Monday night

Son,

I am so sorry about the speech Bush has just given to the nation.
I believe by now you are aware of the forty-eight hour ultimatum
that has been given. It makes me so sad and angry to see that this
government has so unjustly decided to put the lives of all you brave
soldiers in harm's way for what could easily have been worked out
in a peaceful manner. Know that my heart and soul will be with
you at all times no matter what. I have total faith in you and know
that your decisions and actions will be from the heart. It is time
for you also to have total faith in yourself and what you are capable
of doing. Know that thousands of prayers and good thoughts are
being sent your way daily and hourly. Not only by us your family
and friends, but by thousands of people around the world. We pray
for your safety, for the safety of all soldiers, and for the safety of
all the people in Iraq. Know that we are here and don't worry for
a second about us. We just ask that you take care of yourself, so that
you will be joined again soon in better days. I am here and will take
good care of your mom as she awaits your return. I love you with
all my heart and soul. I send you all the blessings of your father who
will be here peacefully fighting for your safe return. Be safe, listen
to your heart, breathe…and feel the love that is going your way.

Love,
Dad

Tuesday, March 18, 2003
Subject: RE: Monday night

Well guys here we go. We just launched eight of our helos to advanced bases on the border of Iraq. I was left behind only to be told to be ready at a moment's notice to pack up and leave. This is going to be a war. There is no way around it now. The decision is out of our hands, and now God only knows what is going to happen. It was really weird and emotional saying goodbye to all my fellow Marines today. I can't even imagine what is going through their heads. Anyone who says they aren't scared is wrong. I don't know if it is just the waiting that is killing me or the thoughts of how many lives we are going to lose over this. My spirits are high and I know I will be OK. War is ugly and I wish there was another way around this. Now, if you don't hear from me now, it's either I went landside or they cut all communication on the boat. It's bad enough not being able to be with the people you love, but no contact at all is going to be hard. If I go down, it's not for something I believed in. All this glory and medals mean nothing. The only thing I am going to get out of this is to be grateful. I owe you guys both a lot and I am so glad to have you as my parents. I love you and always will.

Your loving Son,
Eric

...Eric Salazar

BASIC TRAINING

Basic Training, Day 1
Drill Sergeant Manchester gives everyone in the platoon
  a 5x7 index card
Says to write down the top three reasons we enlisted
So we can look at it when the training gets tough and
  motivate ourselves
I write down my first reason—I want to serve my country
I try to think of other reasons, my mind draws a blank
I think back to the posters in front of my recruiter's office
I think about the rack of brochures in my local public library
I think of the reasons my new battle-buddies had given
I scribble "college money" and "adventure" but feel like a liar
We tape our cards up in our wall lockers
The next day I add a quote that I'd seen in the chow hall
"I've always admired the ability to bite off more than one can
  chew and then chew it"

Basic Training, Week 2
I've bitten off more than I can chew
Wearing our Kevlars for the first time, my brain feels like
  it's choking
Damn! This thing is heavy!
We're training on how to use the bayonet
It's hot
I'm exhausted
Every pore on my body drips sweat
KILL!!!
We're supposed to yell that every time we execute a move
KILL!!!
It feels good to yell that, focusing and channeling my energy
KILL!!!
Half a decade of sullen teenage angst expelled from my lungs
KILL!!!

I can almost feel the hair growing on my chest
KILL!!!
I no longer mind the heat, the sweat, or the weight of my Kevlar
KILL!!!
Drill Sergeant Corbett leads us in call-and-response:
What makes the green grass grow?
BLOOD BLOOD BRIGHT RED BLOOD
What makes the pretty flowers bloom?
GUTS GUTS GRITTY GRIMY GUTS
What are the two types of bayonet fighters?
THE QUICK AND THE DEAD
Who are we?
THE QUICK
Who are they?
THE DEAD
What is the purpose of the bayonet?
TO KILL! KILL! KILL WITHOUT MERCY!

...Sholom Keller

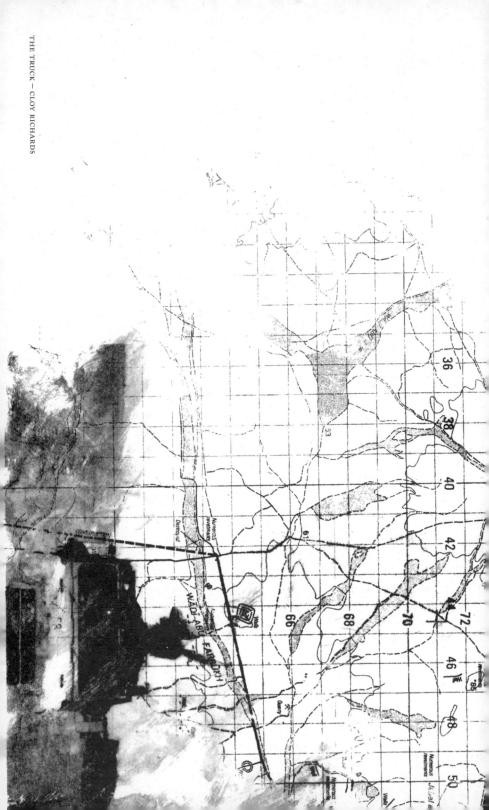

THAT DAMN TRUCK

It was just a truck. A big, green truck. Not a pickup or a big rig, but a big, green, seven-ton military truck. A big, green truck in a barren, desert wasteland that stuck out like a sore thumb. The cab held two marines, and mounted above the cab was a gunner armed with a Browning M2 .50 caliber machine gun, just like the ones you see pointed out of the sides of helicopters in the movie *Black Hawk Down*. In the bed of the truck were ten severely uncomfortable and easily irritable marines, seated upon 3,000 pounds of explosives and ammunition—the last place you'd want to be if a rocket-propelled grenade happened to come whistling your way. Fistfights would break out over elbow space and legroom. That truck was a cramped death trap where sleep was impossible and comfort was a wish no genie could grant. However, to the boys of First Squad, Alpha Company, it was so much more than a truck.

Everyone had "their spot" in the back of that truck. Sergeants and corporals got first pick of their spots, while privates and lance corporals got last pick. If a private was so lucky as to pick a comfortable spot, it was very possible that a grouchy sergeant would annex it. I never got so lucky. I carried a heavy machine gun so I was blessed with being stuck on the port (left) side in the back of the bed. My staff sergeant's reasoning for that splendid move was so that I could lay down suppressing fire while everyone else dismounted the truck in case of an attack. I think he did it just to torture me. That spot had to be the most uncomfortable spot of them all. "Thanks a lot staff sergeant," I would mutter every time I climbed into the back of that truck. I made the most out of that spot, though. I mushed the sandbags down in front of me to make a mini-dinner table where I could dine on whatever fine, vacuum-sealed meal Uncle Sam would bless me with. No matter what I did, I could never keep the hard, aluminum canisters of explosives from digging right into my buttocks and thighs. Sitting in the back of that truck was a nightmare. I hated that truck.

We rode that truck through a hole in the berm separating Kuwait and Iraq. We led tanks and armored vehicles into Iraq in that truck. I even leaned out of the back of that truck and tried to touch the fire burning off of an oil well in Southern Iraq. I waved to young Iraqi children who would give me a thumb up and yell "America good" as I passed by in that truck. In the back of that truck I day-dreamed of what my ex-girlfriend was doing back home and who she was doing it with. I shot snipers off rooftops from the back of that truck. Our driver would tell all of us in the back when we were about to run over an enemy so we could all be quiet and listen for the sound of the crunch of his bones under the weight of American steel and once we heard it we would all cheer, in the back of that truck. I killed my first person in the back of that truck. I hated myself in that truck.

The weather was unusually mild on March 25th, 2003, in South-central Iraq. There was a cool breeze that made our nuclear, biological, chemical protective suits actually a bit manageable

in that miserable desert. We had been stuck in that truck for three days straight and were growing irritable, but that breeze was just the reprieve we needed to stop our bitter grumbling. It was just a calm before the storm. The rain clouds rolled in so fast it was like God had dimmed the lights in Iraq. As the first raindrops bounced off the barrel of my machine gun I heard thunder clap nearby and searched the sky for lightning. I looked out the back of the truck and saw the truck behind us explode and realized that wasn't thunder I was hearing.

"Fall out, fall out," our staff sergeant screamed as my squad poured out of the truck. Some snipers were taking potshots at my boys while they were jumping out of the truck so I laid down suppressing fire. I was in the perfect spot in the back of the truck to mow every sniper down. "Thanks a lot staff sergeant," I thought to myself. I still hate that spot in the truck.

TRUCK PHOTOS BY CLOY RICHARDS

After I jumped out of the truck I could see what was in front of us, even though I didn't want to. The vehicles in front of us had been blown apart, including the captain's vehicle. Before I ran to my position on the perimeter I tried to catch a glimpse of the damage but could only focus on the captain and the bloody stump where his arm used to be. I was stunned by this gruesome sight but quickly regained a grasp on the situation after I watched my captain tie a dressing around his own wound, pull out his pistol and scream "Let's get these sons of bitches!" I lay in the mud for 18 hours shooting whoever dare breach my section of the perimeter. We were outnumbered 3,000 to 150 but after all was said and done, most of us climbed back into those trucks. Thirteen of us had jumped off that truck earlier that morning. Eight of us climbed back in that night. I had missed that truck.

To this day, I can't put my finger on what was so special about that truck. It was so cramped, so uncomfortable. I wouldn't get back into that truck for a million dollars. Yet after that rainy day in the desert, I had never been happier to get in that truck, and I prayed I would never have to get out ever again. Unfortunately there were a lot more days like March 25th, 2003, and every time we climbed back into that truck there were fewer of us. That never made it more comfortable. Those of us who were left would stuff ourselves into our old positions so as not to interfere with the space a fallen comrade had once occupied. That truck offered so much pain, so much grief and yet, so much comfort. No one ever died inside that truck. It was only when we got out of the truck, it seemed, when our brothers would die. I miss that truck.

...Cloy Richards

WHEN I PRAYED

when I prayed to the president
my eyes were sewn closed
I thought of the girl on the street corner
and how she was exposed
by the sun, the dust, the gun
breaking and beating over seas of sound

when I prayed to the president
my hands were tied
barbed-wire skin like shards of shrapnel
a rope of lies
burned by broken street signs
and yellow ribbons paid for in pain

when I prayed to the president
I was reaching from the soil
growing like the palm groves
that choke from the taste of oil
my mouth stuck from tar and territory
I drew "S.O.S." in the mud

but when it rained we were as tall as buildings
drunk with concussions and broken asphalt
and we were young
and in love
with ourselves

...Phil Aliff

BLOOD BADGES

I was a private in basic training when I received my first blood.

We qualified on our rifles and that night the senior drill sergeant lined us up. He told us of the importance of our accomplishment, that we had earned it but still had yet to receive our honor. I stood chest out, a soldier on each side grabbing my arms. He grinned before he pounded the metal sharpshooter pin into my chest. It felt good. None of us wore our shirts that night; we compared our uniformed skin.

My next was when I was promoted in the field on deployment to Twentynine Palms, California. My platoon was especially bored, so everyone got a chance to drive my PV2[1] rank into my collarbone. I received my PFC[2] and Specialist rank the same way, always taking the opportunity to bestow the honor on my fellow lower ranking soldiers. I was promoted to Sergeant in Iraq. The rest of the NCOs[3] who felt the need gave me a firm handshake and a collar pound "Welcome to the corps"—gauntlet style. My upper chest was a scatter of trickling blood and penetration. It always healed quickly, even without care. I still wear that rank; I let them pound it so deep that I may never pull it out of my skin.

...Drew Cameron

---

[1] Private Second Class

[2] Private First Class

[3] Non-Commissioned Officers

THE SEXUAL POLITICS OF WAR

Part 1:
    Leave the vehicle and look around closely
    Make sure no one is ready to attack you
    Turn the corner, look behind you and around the corner
    Make sure no one is waiting to attack you
    Approach the door and check if anyone is inside
    Make sure no one is waiting to attack you
    Close the door so no one will enter behind you
    Ready to attack you
    Enter into the building, look all around
    Make sure no one is waiting to attack you
    Keep calm when someone appears should they be
      more than just walking by
    Realize you are not breathing
    Relax
    Take a deep breath
    War
    Is it a place young men, targets in uniform,
      fight in a far off land
    Or is it my walk home at night, womanhood,
      my uniform and target

Part 2:
    Are we so different?
    The warrior and the woman
    Stay in your place
    One fights their wars
    One cleans their kitchens
    Both should just shut up and listen
    Don't ask any questions

Fight the good fight
Same war on different fronts
So far in front we are facing each other

Part 3:
Is this your choice or our lack of choices?

...Jen Hogg

ME AND MY RIFLE

Why did I like carrying an M-16? I waited in line with the others
in Basic Training like it was Christmas morning. It's strange to
think about now but I can tell you I was elated to receive the
famous M-16. All the movies and video games never showed me
what it truly was. During my time in the Army, I finally understood
what a rifle was all about. It's a tool of death. Never has it created
something, or fixed a problem. It doesn't spread democracy.
It doesn't spread peace. A rifle crack is quick, sharp and final.

Now that I have acknowledged that the M-16 is far from a toy
I again ask why? I have to be honest. I loved carrying a rifle. After
awhile it fused into my skin, bones, character and soul. Am I evil
for that? Am I a violent monster? Well let me tell you something,
I came from an average all-American family. My mom is a school-
teacher. Our walls are filled with pictures of little league, vacations,
grandkids, high school and weddings. I open doors for little old
ladies. Yes, I can safely say that I'm American and I loved the M-16.
If I'm a normal lower middle-class lad, then something is wrong.
Why did I know the difference between an M-16 and an AK-47
before I could compare a Hindu to a Muslim, or a sonnet to a Haiku?

...Nathan Lewis

BITING THE BULLET

A stupid war photo. Josh thought it up, "Biting the bullet." Ha ha, right? But with a civilian's eyes, I think, "What the fuck?" An out-post, interstate highway in the background, and an M240 machine gun within arm's reach. Hours were spent in the hundred-degree heat on that roof. I notice there is a pair of flex-cuffs on my left shoulder. How many of those did I use over there?

A pen is in my sleeve pocket; I was such a dutiful RTO.[1] Always ready. The CLS[2] bag on my left hip. Who knew that only a few months later, that would be used on Doc Wagner. Sweat stains cover my IBA.[3] Oil and dirt mix dark and nasty.

PHOTO BY MATT HRUTKAY

And, finally, the climax: an M203 round in my teeth. I didn't think at the time that that thing has a five-meter kill radius. Though perfectly safe, if it was armed, there would be no more sunglasses, no more flex-cuffs, no more name tape. Only a hole in the roof dripping with yours and Josh's blood and bones.

...Matt Hrutkay

---

[1] Radio Transmission Operator
[2] Combat Life Saver
[3] Interceptor Ballistic Armor

DEADLY DAYS

As a young boy growing up, I remember playing "Army" with my brother and friends for hours upon hours, days at a time. It seems as though in our country kids grow up with a gun in their hands—either that or watching movies and playing video games involving deadly weapons and killing. I guess this sort of childhood "fantasy" came true four and a half years ago when I volunteered to join the United States Marine Corps. I was trained non-stop for months upon months by the Corps for one specific reason: to become a professional killer. Even through these miserable days of relentless training, which included instant blister-forming fifteen-mile hikes, sleeping in sand for weeks at a time, and shooting over a hundred thousand rounds in the hot California sun, these daily tasks still did not prepare me for when that day finally came—when I had to take another human being's life.

It was an unusually chilly night for Iraq. I was sitting on a plastic lawn chair in our wooden shack we call a "C-Hut." This twelve-foot by twelve-foot room was my home for seven months in the summer and winter of 2004-2005. I suddenly heard the raspy voice of our squad leader Sgt. Abernathy scream: "Saddle up, boys." Now this was supposed to be our day of rest, our "off" time. No one was particularly happy that we were about to do anything at this godawful hour of the night. A couple of buddies and I started loading the wood into our armored trucks, all the while smoking cigarettes and complaining about our upcoming excursion. These were always the worst missions—middle of the night, unexpected, little preparation. No one was in a jovial mood by any means. After rounding up the guys, loading the trucks, and receiving our mission statement, we hit the road.

The outpost, called the "RE-TRANS site," was a good twenty-minute drive from the main base. The ride seemed like an eternity. However, I can't say our particular Humvee and its personnel were in poor spirits. I had my CD player and headphones on.

PFC[1] Glasper, who was an African-American kid from the inner city of Chicago, was up in the turret gun on top of our vehicle with the same goofy smile and lost look on his face as he had for most of the deployment. Lance Corporal Villa, a Mexican friend of mine from Southern Texas, was behind the wheel as always. Villa is truly a great spirit, rarely in a bad mood and willing to talk about anything. It didn't matter that it was the middle of the night; the jokes kept coming as if it were Villa's job to be as sarcastic as possible. I thoroughly enjoyed sharing a vehicle with these two gentlemen during our stay in the desert. It turned out to be a safe trip to our destination; we dropped off the supplies and had a chance to smoke and joke with some buddies of ours from the second squad. I suddenly heard the Humvees starting. Time to hit the road and head back to base!

Every time we drove at night, Iraq looked so much prettier—no blindingly bright sun or hot desert floor, just the endless stars in the night sky and all its wonderful beauty. The moon was spectacular, full and bright as ever. I remember thinking this almost every time I looked out the window on that drive home. I faded asleep fast from this sight and from the melody in my ear. I know this probably doesn't sound like the most vigilant thing to do while driving around in a combat zone, but I figured we'd taken this route a thousand times, I might as well catch up on some much-needed sleep time.

I was awoken by the two deafening gun shots. It was Sgt. Abernathy, "GO, GO, and GO," he screamed at the top of his lungs, and pointed wildly in the direction of a field off to the left side of the road. Villa frantically asked, "Do you see anything? DO YOU SEE ANYTHING?" Louder and louder each time, with the response being the same, not a thing in sight. WHAM! We hit a deep ditch going about forty miles per hour, my weapon turned around and the plastic hand-guard to protect my skin from the red-hot barrel busted off. PFC Glasper took the hit hard; he was crunched over in the back seat of the truck in the fetal position from having his rib cage smashed against the roof. I finally caught a glimpse of a silhouette. It was a man running and in a flash of a second he was gone—he jumped down into a drainage ditch. Villa stopped the Humvee, and I quickly exited the vehicle. All I could think while approaching the ditch was, "Please do not pop up and shoot me in the face, please do not pop up and shoot me." I looked down but couldn't see a thing. BANG, BANG, BANG ... I emptied my entire magazine of rounds into the ditch. I couldn't stop pulling the trigger, and I even stopped and reloaded another magazine and continued to fire. Villa came running towards me with a flashlight. There he was, dead as dead can be, no more than a couple feet in front of my face. To this day I can't remember why, but when Villa put that light on him I fired two more rounds into his already bloodied corpse—maybe out of fear of him still being alive, or the possibility of me having to care for a man I already had tried to kill. "Check the body for bombs," Sgt. Abernathy shouted as he came running towards the scene. Upon picking up the body, we saw that I had shot the man in the back of the head, resulting in the complete collapse of his skull structure. His forehead also had a baseball-size gaping hole where the bullet exited. There's something sensational about taking another human life. My immediate reaction was that of accomplishment, satisfaction, of being a "hero." Overwhelming, that was the sense I had at the time. Not sure whether to cry or let out a primal scream.

I soon found out that the man had three accomplices, all of whom were attempting to plant a roadside bomb on the path we were traveling. When the explosive experts arrived, they told us that if we had gotten there a couple minutes later we would have never disrupted them, and one of our trucks would have been blown to pieces. The euphoric feeling faded fast. On the way home I felt numb almost-not upset, not excited-almost a sense of complete and utter tranquility. Back at the base we arrived to a small crowd of fellow marines who heard of the news, who congratulated and patted me on the back for what I had done. I remember wanting to get to the showers as fast as possible—maybe cleaning myself would rid my body of this awful energy it was receiving. Still pumped from the adrenaline rush, I thought showering was the best option. The entire rest of that night, I felt as if he were watching my every step, lurking around every corner, perched under every stair. I hadn't felt such fear since I was a young boy. Attempting to wind down the night, I was on the porch of our shack having a smoke. Vick, a quiet guy from a Southern Baptist family of Kentucky, came out to talk to me. "Pretty crazy we ran into those guys out there … how you feeling man?" I didn't know what to say—I mean, how did I feel? I was happy we didn't die, yet I was extremely upset that someone had to die in the end. I said I was fine, and we talked about how it's a part of war and how I did the right thing. I told him I always wondered what it was like to take another human being's life, and now I know.

Unfortunately this wasn't the last time I had to discharge my weapon in self-defense during our tour in Iraq. Two days later we were ambushed, and my best friend and platoon member was killed in a five-hour firefight with insurgents. Maybe this was part of life. Maybe this was God's way of showing me what it was like to have a life so close to me taken so fast. I found out really quickly what killing and the tragedies of war were like, all within seventy-two hours. There are a million ways to describe a war: unneeded, useless, tragic, horrific … I would also say missing and sad. Missing is a piece of me that I will never ever get back. Sad is the state of affairs in the world in which we live in today. That piece of me and that empty sadness that fills my heart is and forever will be in Iraq and in my memory.

...Vince Emanuele

---

[1] Private First Class

STRUCTURED CRUELTY:
LEARNING TO BE A LEAN, MEAN KILLING MACHINE

I will never forget standing in formation after the end of our final "hump"—Marine-speak for a forced march—at the end of the Crucible in March, 1997. The Crucible is the final challenge during the United States Marine Corps boot camp: a two-and-a-half day, physically exhausting exercise in which sleep deprivation, scarce food, and a series of obstacles test teamwork and toughness. The formidable nine-mile stretch ended with our ascent up the "Grim Reaper," a small mountain in the hilly terrain of Camp Pendleton, California. As we stood at attention, the Commanding Officer made his way though our lines, inspecting his troops and giving each of us an eagle, globe, and anchor pin, the mark of our final transition from recruit to Marine. But what I recall most was not the pain and exhaustion that filled every ounce of my trembling body, but the sounds that surrounded me as I stood at attention with eyes forward.

Mixed in with the refrain of Lee Greenwood's "God Bless the USA" belting from a massive sound system were the soft and gentle sobs emanating from numerous newborn marines. Their cries stood in stark contrast to the so-called "warrior spirit" we had earned and now came to epitomize. While some may claim that these unmanly responses resulted from a patriotic emotional fit or even out of a sense of pride in being called "Marine" for the very first time, I know that for many the moisture streaming down our cheeks represented something much more anguished and heartrending.

What I learned about Marines is that despite the stereotype of the chivalrous knight, wearing dress blues with sword drawn, or the green killing machine that is always "ready to rumble," the young men and women I encountered instead represented a cross-section of working-class America. There were neither knights nor machines among us. During my five years in active-duty service, I befriended a recovering meth addict who was still "using"; a young male who had prostituted himself to pay his rent before he signed up; a Salvadoran immigrant serving in order to receive a green card; a single mother who could not afford her child's health care needs as a civilian; a gay teenager who entertained our platoon by singing Madonna karaoke in the barracks to the delight of us all; and many of the country's poor and poorly educated. I came to understand very well what those cries on top of the Grim Reaper expressed. Those teardrops represented hope in the promise of a change in our lives from a world that, for many of us as civilians, seemed utterly hopeless.

Marine Corps boot camp is a thirteen-week training regimen unlike any other. According to the USMC's recruiting website, "Marine recruits learn to use their intelligence … and to live as upstanding moral beings with real purpose."[1] Yet if teaching intelligence and morals are the stated purpose of its training, the Corps has a peculiar way of implementing its pedagogy. In reality, its educational method is based on a planned and structured form of cruelty. I remember my first visit to the "chow-hall" in which three drill instructors (DIs), wearing their signature "Smokey Bear" covers, pounced upon me for having looked at them, screaming that I was a "Nasty Piece of Civilian Shit." From then on, I learned that you could only look at a DI when instructed to by the command "Eyeballs!" In addition, recruits could only speak in the third person, thus ridding our vocabulary of the term "I" and divorcing ourselves from our previous civilian identities.

Our emerging group mentality was built upon and reinforced by tearing down and degrading us through a series of regimented and ritualistic exercises in the first phase of boot camp. Despite having an African-American and a Latino DI, recruits in my platoon were ridiculed with derogatory language that included racial epithets. But recruits of color were not the only victims: We were all "fags," "pussies," and "shitbags." We survived through a twisted sort of leveling based on what military historian Christian G. Appy calls a "solidarity of the despised."[2]

We relearned how to execute every activity, including the most personal aspects of our hygiene. While eating, we could only use our right hand while our left had to stay directly on our knee, and our eyes had to stare directly at our food trays. Our bathroom breaks were so brief that three recruits would share a urinal at a time so that the entire platoon of sixty-three recruits could relieve themselves in our minute-and-half time limit. On several occasions, recruits soiled their uniforms during training. Every evening, DIs inspected our boots for proper polish and our belt buckles for satisfactory shine while we stood at attention in our underwear. Then, we would "mount our racks" (bunk beds), lie at attention, and scream all three verses of the Marine Corps hymn at the top of our lungs. While the DIs would proclaim that these inspections were to insure that our bodies had not been injured during training, I suspect that there were ulterior motives as well. These examinations were attempts to indoctrinate us with an emerging military masculinity that is based on male sexuality linked to respect for the uniform and a fetishization of combat.

After the playing of Taps, lights went out, at which time, a DI would circle around the room and begin moralizing. "One of these days, you're going to figure out what's really tough in the world," he would exclaim. "You think you've got it so bad. But in recruit training, you get three meals a day while we tell you when to shit and blink," he continued. The DI would then lower his voice, "But when you're out on your own, you're gonna see what's hard. You'll see what tough is when you knock up your old woman. You'll realize what's cruel when you get married and find yourself stuck with a fat bitch who just squats out ungrateful kids. You'll learn what the real world's about when you're overseas and your wife back in the states robs you blind and sleeps with your best friend." The DI's nightly homiletic speeches, full of an unabashed hatred of women, were part of the second phase of boot camp: the process of rebuilding recruits into Marines.

The process of reconstructing recruits and molding them into future troops is based on building a team that sees itself in opposition to those who are outside of it. After the initial shock of the first phase of training, DIs indoctrinate recruits to dehumanize the enemy in order to train them on how to overcome any fear or prejudice against killing. In fact, according to longtime counter-recruitment activist Tod Ensign, the military has deliberately researched how to best design training to teach recruits how to kill. Such research was needed because humans are instinctively reluctant to kill. Dr. Dave Grossman disclosed in his work, *On Killing*, that fewer than twenty percent of U.S. troops fired their weapons in World War II during combat. As a result, the military reformed training standards so that more soldiers would pull their trigger against the enemy. Grossman credits these training modifications for the transformation of the Armed Forces in the Vietnam War, in which ninety to ninety-five percent of soldiers fired their weapons. These reforms in training were based on teaching recruits how to dehumanize the enemy.[3]

The process of dehumanization is central to military training. During Vietnam, the enemy in Vietnam was simply a "gook," a "dink," or a "slope."[4] Today, "rag head" and "sand nigger" are the racist epithets lodged against Arabs and Muslims. After every command, we would scream, "Kill!" But our call for blood took on particular importance during our physical training, when we learned how to fight with pugil sticks, wooden sticks with padded ends: how to run an obstacle course with fixed bayonets; or how to box and engage in hand-to-hand combat. We were told to imagine the "enemy" in all of our combat training, and it was always implied that the "enemy" was of Middle Eastern descent. "When some rag head comes lurking up from behind, you're gonna give 'em ONE," barked the training DI. We all howled in unison, "Kill!" Likewise, when we charged toward the dummy on an obstacle course with our fixed bayonets, it was clear to all that the lifeless form was Arab.

Even in 1997, we were being brainwashed to accept the coming Iraq War. Abruptly interrupting a class, one of numerous courses we attended on military history, first aid, and survival skills, a Series Chief DI excitedly announced that all training was coming to a halt.

We were to be shipped immediately to the Gulf, because Saddam had just fired missiles into Israel. Given that we lived with no knowledge of the outside world, with neither TV nor newspapers, and that we experienced constant high levels of stress and a discombobulating environment, the DI's false assertion seemed all too believable. After a half-hour panic, we were led out of the auditorium to face the rebuke and scorn of our platoon DIs. It turned out that the interruption was a skit planned to scare us into the realization that we could face war at any moment. The trick certainly had the planned effect on me, as I pondered what the hell I had gotten myself into. I also now realize that we were being indoctrinated with schemes for war in the Middle East. Our hatred of the Arab "other" was crafted from the very beginning of our training through fear and hate.

Almost ten years since I stood on the yellow footprints that greet new recruits at the Marine Corps Recruit Depot in San Diego, I express gratitude for my luck during my enlistment. I was fortunate never to have witnessed a day of combat and was honorably discharged months after 9/11. However, joining the military is like playing Russian roulette. With wars raging in Iraq and Afghanistan, and the likelihood of military action against Iran, troops in the Corps today face grimmer odds. In these "dirty wars," troops cannot tell friend from foe, leading to war crimes against a civilian population. Our government is cynically promoting a campaign of lies and deception to justify its illegal actions—with the complicity of both parties in Washington—and our troops are fighting to support regimes that lack popular support and legitimacy.

With nearly 4,000 U.S. troops now dead and thousands more maimed and crippled, I look back to the other young men I heard sobbing on that sunny winter morning on top of the Reaper. The reasons we enlisted were as varied as our personal histories. Yet, it is the starkest irony that the hope we collectively expressed for a better life may have indeed cost us our very lives. When one pulls the trigger called "enlistment," he or she faces the gambling chance of experiencing war, conflicts that inevitably lead to the degradation of the human spirit.

The war crimes committed by U.S. troops in Iraq—such as the brutality exhibited at Mahmoudiya, in which soldiers allegedly gang-raped a teenage Iraqi girl and burned her body to destroy the evidence—are, in fact, part and parcel of all imperialist wars. The USMC's claim that recruits learn "to live as upstanding moral beings with real purpose" is a sickening ploy aimed to disguise its true objectives. Given the fact that Marines are molded to kill the enemy "other" from TD (training day) One combined with the bestial nature of colonial war, it should come as no surprise that rather than turning "degenerates" into paragons of virtue, the Corps is more likely transforming men into monsters.

And yet, as much as these war crimes reveal about the conditions of war, the circumstances facing an occupying force, and the peculiar brand of Marine training, they also reflect a bitter truth about the civilian world in which we live. It speaks volumes that in order for young working-class men and women to gain self-confidence or self-worth, they seek to join an institution that trains them how to destroy, maim, and kill. The desire to become a Marine—as a journey to one's manhood or as a path to self-improvement—is a stinging indictment of the pathology of our class-ridden world.

...Martin Smith

[1] "Recruit Training—Accepting The Challenge," *Marines*, August 5, 2006; <http://www.marines.com/page/usmc. jsp?pageId=/page/Detail-XML-Conversion.jsp?pageName=The-Crucible&flashRedirect=true>.

[2] Christian G. Appy, "Military Training: Basic Training," in *America's Military Today: The Challenge of Militarism*, ed. Tod Ensign (New York: New Press, 2004), 50.

[3] Lt. Col. Dave Grossman, *On Killing* (Boston: Little, Brown and Company, 1995), 250–51.

[4] David Roediger, "Gook: the short history of an Americanism," in *Towards the Abolition of Whiteness: Essays on Race, Politics, and Working-Class History* (London: Verso, 1994).

Mere words cannot atone
for my transgressions

But words are all I have

Over and over again
I can only say I'm sorry

Sorry for my silence
Your silence is deafening in my soul

Sorry for my cowardess
I am a coward not to speak
I'm sorry for everything
Forgive me brother, forgive me sister
Forgive me father
for I have sinned...

SORRY – MIKE BLAKE

THE RADIO

When I was in Mrs. Riner's junior English class at MacArthur High School, we were required to read a short story titled "The Radio." The plot was simple: A couple in the 1930s was given a magical radio that allowed them to hear all their neighbors' conversations. They were at first elated, but ultimately haunted by the miracle of their ability. They could hear all the horrors of society that usually go unnoticed or are covered up and sterilized ... and they couldn't turn it off, and they couldn't change the channel. It took seven years, but I eventually went back to that story in my head and felt their horror.

August 24th, 2006, was a routine day for my squad in Baghdad. We had gone to Traffic Headquarters and I had gotten to visit with Ali, my little Iraqi friend. With business taken care of, we started to make the familiar trek back to Camp Liberty. It was a hot day, over 120 degrees, and I stood up just a little higher than usual with my sleeves unbuttoned to let the air circulate inside my body armor and clothing. It had been a good day.

Back on Route Irish, we were on the home stretch when the call came out over the radio:

"Eagle Dustoff, Eagle Dustoff, this is Red Knight seven over"
"This is Eagle Dustoff, over"
"Eagle Dustoff, I need MEDEVAC;[1] my gunner has been shot by a sniper."

The voice went on to recite the nine-line MEDEVAC report and I marveled at how cool, calm, and collected he sounded. My squad leader plotted the grid coordinates and found that this had occurred only a couple blocks away from one of our two main destinations on Market Road.

"Cliburn, go ahead and get down; someone might be aiming at your melon right now," Cpt.[2] Ray said. Sergeant Bruesch concurred and

GOD-F

You see yet it no longer fazes:
Burning bodies,
Wasted ammo cases,
Too far removed within your living-room,
Your palace-tomb.

Fucked-up nation:
Your children die by the moment,
Yet you write it off as bravery,
Because you are too cowardly to call it
what it really is:
Nation-sanctioned suicide.

Buluc Chabtan[1] has reawakened,
Ares[2] is once again running free,
The old war gods are in full swing,
And at the end of the day,
Death and violence rule supreme.

...Raymond Camper

---

[1] Buluc Chabtan was the Mayan god of War. He was also seen and worshipped as
the god of Violence, Human Sacrifices (which were made to him), and the cause for
any unexplained sudden death or deaths.

[2] Ares was the Olympian god of war (known as Mars to the Romans), and was seen
as the god of savage war, of bloodlust. Ares was slaughter personified.

APOLOGIES
MEMORY
GUILT
ALL THESE MEMORIES NOT HOW I WANTED NOT HOW I WANT THEM
MEMORIES ARE DREAMS AND LIES IF I STILL BELIEVE MYTH AND NARRATIVES OF YOUTH
AND LOVE AND GOD AND LIES AND FRIENDS WE THINK WHAT WE WANT TO THINK
NARRATIVES / STORIES OF HOW WE THINK WHAT WE WANT TO THINK
I WANT TO THINK OF ME GOOD
BUT FOOD WAS A MYTH THAT IS NOT A MEMORY OF GUILT
GUILT OF. NOT EVEN A SHIT FOR THE THOUSANDS UPON THE ROAD
DAMN HADJI
ALL ASK FOR FOOD ON LONG DRIVE
OLD MAN AND SPOILED BELLY OF FAT NARRATIVES OF PEACE COMPLACENCY
MEMORIES ARE NOT MYTHS / GRAY AND CONFUSED
DRIVE ROAD
APOLOGIES
APOLOGIES AND SUNRISE ON NO SLEEP THE PIRATE BOMBS
AND GUILT
GUILT
DUST OF BEAUTIES PAIN OF SOMEONES LIFE
SOME PEOPLES LIFE
DAMN HADJI...
SUNRISE
SUN UP
SON SET ON MEMORIES OF
NOT THE NARRATIVES OF MYTHS
OF LIFE I THOUGHT WAS ME...

BELONGS NOWHERE

APOLOGIES — AARON HUGHES

EVERY SOLDIER'S FEAR

My luck had been pretty good so far in Iraq, but on this day it had run out. We all knew we could get hit with it at any time. Living in constant fear of it, our stomachs tightened and pulses raced at the mere mentioning of it. Every day you wake up and wonder to yourself, will this be the day? Any time you see black smoke and flames you assume the worst. My driver and I had gone three months in Iraq without getting hit with it, but this brutally hot, brown-colored sky day in May 2003 we finally got it. Shit-burning detail. It was our turn.

"Lewis and Guthrie, you're on shit-burning detail," barked our platoon sergeant from the front of formation. Other instructions were given out for the day, and on the command of "fall out," soldiers broke in all directions to begin the missions of the day. Desperately we tried to trade duties with others. We tried to switch with Cox and Blea for the lead truck in the convoy into Baghdad. They politely refused. We even tried switching duties with two new guys in the guard tower. No go. We were stuck with it. You may ask, "What is shit-burning detail?" SBD for short—the Army loves acronyms.

SBD is the Army's answer to the problem of disposing of human waste in an area with no running water or sewer system. Urine (number one) is a no brainer: PVC pipes carry liquid waste down into the ground and away forever but this isn't done with number two. Number two cannot be just dumped into a hole. Imagine the pile that would result from two to three thousand soldiers every day, not to mention a month or more. It is unclear exactly when the Army first started using SBD, but it must have been around the time they started using diesel and gasoline-powered motors. The first thing you do for SBD is collect supplies: Twenty gallons diesel, five gallons gas, two pair heavy leather gloves, one long metal pole—preferably over ten feet—and something to tie over your face.

Next you need to pull the waste barrels from beneath the latrines. This is done very cautiously with constant and violent cursing. Once the barrels have been moved a safe distance away they are placed in a row. Depending on the size of your unit there could be five or fifty barrels. We had twenty. One gallon of diesel is then poured into each barrel along with a splash of gasoline on top as an accelerator. Now you're ready to fire it up. Be careful though, this is where it gets rough. Your mixture is now basically napalm, extremely explosive and dangerous. The best way to avoid singed hair and burns is to stuff gas soaked rags into one end of the pole and use it as a giant match. This is the way we decided to light our sick firestorm. The gasoline fumes ignited by the rag quickly ignited the diesel fuel and shit mixture, beginning the long, slow burn. Once the six-foot flames die down, you must constantly stir the mixture with your pole. This is where the length of the pole is important. Size does matter. Now all you can do is wait and occasionally add a splash of diesel to keep the fire going. Even while standing upwind with a cloth over your face, it is hard to avoid the smell. The smoke is absorbed into your clothes and drifts across the desert in low, black clouds. A full barrel will take about three hours to burn down to gray ash. The barrels are then allowed to cool and placed back into the latrine. You also have to remember to watch the latrines while the barrels are out because you don't want to deal with the mess of someone using a latrine without a barrel underneath. Trust me, they will try.

Styles and technique may vary, but that is basically SBD. There are many veterans from many wars that have had this excruciating and terrible duty, and it is one that is seared into my memory. This was the type of day that convinced me not to reenlist in the Army. No thanks, you can take your $40,000 bonus and shove it. There has got to be a better way.

...Nathan Lewis

FAIR EXCHANGE

"Mistah, mistah, gimme mistah," he begs for food, money, sunglasses, ammunition. He entertains with "M-4 Haji Killer" pointing to our weapons. "240 Bravo, Bad Mutha Fucka." When the NCOs turn away we buy whiskey, porn, hash. Why doesn't he beg for a clean home, a new school, a safe ball field? Because he knows he will never get these things from a US soldier. "M-4 Haji Killer" We laugh and buy whiskey.

FAIR EXCHANGE – GARETT REPPENHAGEN

MARINES

standing here with wind blasting against my face
standing on the edge of my mind is such a romantic place
tears running down like a thunderstorm with my thoughts
  screaming inside the silence
I stare at the stars and ponder if what was what and
  who would really win
this pain this disgust this sin
fuck the world because it is just going to happen again
I hold on to your memories like a lifesaver in a drowning sea
I beg God for answers but He chooses to let me be
My voice is quiet and my emotions so raw
no one can really understand unless they saw
to all my brothers
we will always be together
to all my friends gone
this world is just a bump in the road
I will be there soon it won't take long
we went to hell
and some are still there
Call me day or night and you know I will be there
to the families still at a loss even though no one left
this is the shit that feels so heavy on us all
because you might not have legs to walk
but forever stand tall
work and life and remains linger
I am allowed to have my opinions but I will break the finger
of the hand that points
and there is no point but the point is that exactly

...Greg Strehl

I AM WHO SURVIVED

I am a Christian
Who survived nine Commandments but violated one
Thou shalt not kill
Plain and simple, right?
It's more complicated than that
I followed my leaders with a long black crucifix in my hands.
I loaded Proverbs into magazines and shot them out of my crucifix
I carried Bibles in my grenade pouches.
Forgive me Father, for I have sinned
I have allowed bearers of false witness to burn You in an oil fire
I have allowed false idols to drop You on innocent victims,
   killing some, and disfiguring others
I have killed and allowed killing
I shall never kill again
I shall never get lost in the sandstorm of lies and shoot my way out.
Who survived?
I might have, but my faith didn't

...Cloy Richards

EVERYTHING WAS DEAD AND DYING.

Kelly Dougherty

SOMETIMES YOU WONDER
HOW ANYTHING COULD GROW AT ALL.

Mike Blake

we shall sta
You, are not my
We will clan

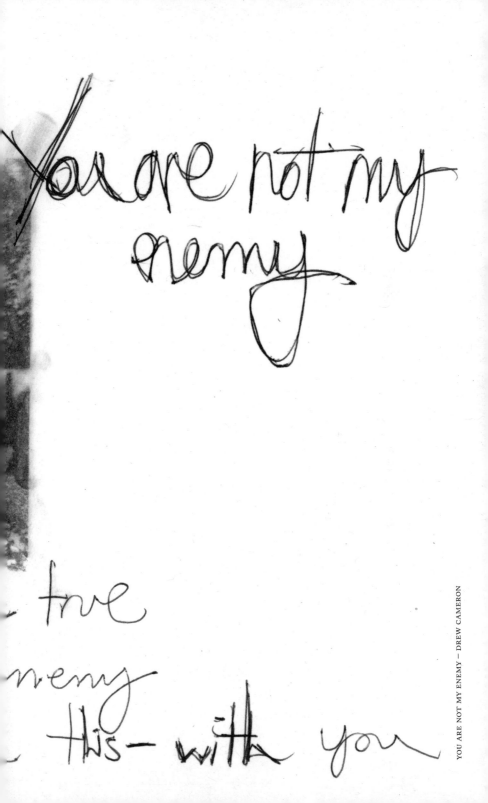

You are not my
enemy

... true

nemy

... this— with you

YOU ARE NOT MY ENEMY

You are not my enemy
my brother my sister,
but I have done something wrong
and perhaps I am now yours.
I went to your home,
I went inside,
soiled your rug and
bullied your children.

You are not my enemy
my father my mother.
I drove on you,
threw garbage in your window,
burned your garden
and spit in your water.

You are not my enemy
my grandmother my grandfather.
I built walls between us.
Rubble made sound,
sand scattered plastic bags all around
rifles and checkpoints
bright lights into your eyes.

No, you are not my enemy
my partner my friend.
We were betrayed.

You are not my enemy,
my child my self.
Our blood is the same.

You are not my enemy
my memories and rage.
Re-making sense now, together.

You are not my enemy
you never were.
You are a part of me
as I am with you.

You are not my enemy
we shall stay true.

You are not my enemy
we will change this,
with you.

you are not my enemy
are not my enemy
not my enemy
my enemy
enemy

.

...Drew Cameron

ARMORED SHADOW — GARETT REPPENHAGEN

APRIL 2

Bright flash
turn to ash
your names are on the wall
Four birds one stone
One large stone
Four pebbles made up that stone

Don't trip
you just fell
You will not catch yourself
Too early or
too late?
Doesn't matter, you just met your fate
The fate that took your lives and
left you charred and
not able to breathe.
To breathe is to take a breath
hard to do when you're part of death
As part of death, you die,
not just on the outside
but within

On the inside you cannot see within
the eye
let your mind die and turn to
dust
Not rust
rust is still there, you are dust
because of the flame
The flame that took your life
The life you once led
You can't now
You're dead

...Jon Turner

TEN SECONDS

The wind is cold and damp against the flesh of my face; the only exposed skin on my body. My shoulders ache under the strain of a thirty-pound armored vest, the back of my neck grows raw from the constant friction of my rifle's heavy canvas strap. My rotten leather pistol holster constricts my lungs and digs painfully into my ribs, the bruises on my hips grow darker with each jolt against the turret ring. Every few minutes I fall asleep for a moment, perhaps a fraction of a second, awakened only when my chin touches the Kevlar neck guard that is fastened tightly over my throat; I'm the only one in my platoon who still wears it. The inside cloth is oily and slick and brown, coated with two months of sweat and filth. Has it really only been two months? I am utterly exhausted, I think of nothing, my mind is completely vacant.

A shot rings out. I ignore it, I'm so tired I don't even care, and besides, someone is always shooting at something around here. I wish they'd just fucking quit, this is so stupid. Another shot, followed by a few more, a bullet glances off something in the road and screams over my head, the spark remains in my eyes. I am awake now, totally awake, the kind of "awake" that cannot be described and most people never have to experience. It's four in the afternoon right now back home. My friends graduated from high school a few months ago, I was still in basic training. Their faces flash through my mind, I can barely recall them now. I know my mother is thinking of me, can she sense what is happening to her only son? More bullets, closer this time, and these do not glance off the road but fly straight past my face, coming dead on now. I can almost taste their heat, like sitting too close to the fireplace, and the sound of a thousand bullwhips crackling all around me. So this is what it's like! Just what I expected, which in turn surprises me. No fear though, I always thought I'd be afraid, thought I'd be the one to lose it, but there's no time for fear now.

I drop down inside the hull of the Humvee and glance around at the faces of my comrades; they stare at me apprehensively. Someone asks if I've been hit; "No. I'm fine, I'm fine." We're moving swiftly now, the road is uneven. I lose my balance for a moment but catch myself on the "butt strap," a canvas strap which is fastened into the turret for me, the gunner, to sit upon—though I've rarely been allowed to do so. In fourth platoon we stand fully erect with eyes scanning back and forth, 180 degrees from shoulder to shoulder, completely exposed for all the world to see and kill. He's still shooting.

I notice that his weapon is on semi-automatic—they never use semi-automatic—but this one, his aim is true. He means to kill me. I respect him now; it's easy to admire a man like him. After all, he is not like me: a soulless mercenary who kills on a three-year contract, this is his life. He hates me. I cannot hate him, but I must try to kill him. He continues to shoot at me, I wish he'd just run on home like the rest of them.

Them ... how I hate Them, we all do. They are so easy to hate, so vile and treacherous, subhuman even. It's because of them that I am here in the first place. God how I hate every inch of every one of them. We will all fight to the death, we are prepared even to take our own lives rather than to fall into their hands, to be tortured, raped, and humiliated. They thieve and lie and have killed boys who were once my friends. People with whom I used to carry intelligent conversations, laugh with, live with, and when I saw them last I never knew it would be the last. They have transformed my friends from men into cumbersome heaps of cold flesh, no longer anything more than a sanitation problem to be solved with the aid of a plastic bag. The blood and entrails must be scrubbed away with Simple Green and scratch pads. My first true friend in the Army was cleaned up in this way. Thank God I wasn't there; had I seen it I wouldn't be able to remember him as I do now. Always a smile, always a comment worthy of note, always something interesting in mind; a husband and a son. And when he died I didn't even bother to cry—I wanted to, I even tried a little bit, but that was stupid, and wrong. No need to lie to yourself, my friend, you are no longer human and everyone knows it.

Pulling myself up, using the butt strap for leverage, I bring my eyes up just far enough to peer over the lip of the turret ring. Where is this motherfucker? I take a look around … there he is! Not "him" per se, but a tiny flash of light, followed by the report of a rifle and the sound of a bullet striking concrete or metal—I never learned to tell the difference. I look down at the orange handle which will unlock the turret and allow me to swing it around, pointing the machine gun in his direction. No, there is no time for all that, with the way this Humvee's leaning and rocking I'd never be able to do it. The gun alone weighs nearly eighty pounds, it's the old kind, a "fifty cal." Besides, he's standing on the roof of an apartment building, and I imagine a family huddled inside their cramped home. They are poor and the weather is cold so they sleep in the same room, probably without beds. I will not send a score of fifty-caliber bullets into that building, to grind and shred the flesh of three generations with one flick of my pathetic thumb, my thumb that is only eighteen years old. I'm not that inhuman, not that cruel, not yet at least.

No, but I will use my rifle. Now I am ready, now I have a purpose. No longer will I cower inside this armored hull and take whatever he chooses to give me. Now I will give him something, I will take control, I will kill him. I bring the rifle to my shoulder, the same kind my father and uncles carried when they were in the service. What a loathsome object; its black steel and plastic lay cold and lifeless in my hands, much like the corpses it was designed to create, incapable of human warmth. I place the tip of my nose on the charging handle, shut my left eye, and peer into the sight hole.

Now I am in a different world entirely. A still, silent void that has but one entrance. You cannot reach it through meditation or by ingesting some strange plant, not even in death can one find it. This man-made world can be glimpsed only through the sights of a rifle, only when it is pointed at a living thing. Here there is no God, no Hell, no consequences and certainly no remorse, those will all come later. For the time being he and I are completely alone, oblivious to the outside world.

Now the moment of truth. Am I really going to go through with this? Can I? Oh yes, I can, and I will, I must. This man is attacking you and your comrades, it is your duty as the gunner of this vehicle to kill him as soon as possible. This is your time, you are responsible for the lives of these men inside this Humvee. I hope … I know that they would do the same for me. Now I'm nervous, my knees tremble, I feel like a kid who's just been caught stealing. For an instant I can clearly see his bullet coming for me, flying straight toward my face, I vividly imagine the impact. Switch the safety off, take a moment to blink your eyes and breathe. Let me wait and see one more muzzle flash before I strike, let him reveal himself just once more. Oh, what sweet satisfaction I am about to receive! Two months of misery and a lost childhood because of you, damn you, I finally get to kill one of you now. I will use you as the object of my vengeance. This is for everything you have done to my life and to my family, you alone will pay the price, tonight. I think of nothing else now but my own misery and suffering—selfish, I know, to kill a man and not even think about him. Then my wish comes true, I see one last flash of light, he has sealed his fate. Instantly I readjust my hands, he's fairly close so I aim a little lower than usual, just like they taught us at Fort Knox. And now I can feel the trigger. In this moment I think of my father, who always taught me to "squeeze" a trigger, never to "pull" it, so, ever so slightly, I begin to squeeze. The movement of my index finger is barely perceptible to the human eye, it curls inward only millimeters per second;

when the rifle finally discharges it's almost unexpected. A shell casing jingles against the floor, I taste smoke, and the guilty finger now points at no one but me.

My enemy, my peer, a man who I have even come to admire in the last few seconds, stops firing immediately. I raise my cheek from the rifle and look at him. I see him for the first time, nothing more than a black silhouette against a midnight sky, but I see him. He goes down behind the edge of the roof. I never see him again, I never learn his name or his lineage, I never learn what became of him.

Later the next morning, when the patrol is over, after I've refueled the Humvee and dismounted the weapons, I'm congratulated by my friends. I am quiet and expressionless, though I'm not upset, not at all. I sit down alone on my cot and disassemble my rifle, the one I used against my enemy, the brother I never had, the only man who has ever faced me as a natural equal. The smell of the spent bullet is strong, but the weapon is mostly clean—after all it was only one shot. I slide a piece of tissue paper through the barrel with a thin rod and push it back and forth, causing me to smile as I recall some past sexual encounter. Soon the paper is plucked from the breech, bearing its little sunburst of black residue. I wipe off each metal part, coating them with fresh oil, and reassemble them slowly, methodically. This rifle did not fail me in my hour of need; it may have even saved my life. I imagine the next soldier who will carry it after I have gone on, after I have shed this awful uniform forever. Will he ever know of the sin it has committed this night? How many people did you kill before I took you from the rack? I push such thoughts aside and am asleep in a matter of seconds.

...Clifton Hicks

LIFT AWAY YOUR PAIN

We did things to other people. Oh how true that statement is. Funny how torture has been going on for so long. Interesting concept how you go to war and have raised levels of anxiety and stress and you turn to hurting or killing people just to make your day better. Why is it I enjoyed the pain I inflicted on innocent people? People with families and lives to be lived. It's not right. It's not humane. I'm sorry I killed your son today. I thank him for looking into my eyes after he fell to the ground. I'm thankful he didn't die after that first round went through his chest causing him to let go of an unforgettable scream directed toward me. Why did you shoot me, Jon? What did I do? I'm willing to bet a hundred dollars your blood stain is still on the sidewalk outside post alpha. I'm sorry for the pain I have caused you and your family. I'm sorry I killed you. You, I don't even know your name. I'm sorry for the other lives I've ruined. Please lift your head and forgive me.
I am no longer the monster I once was.

...Jon Turner

How happy they were the day they raided a Ba'ath Party printing press as they approached Baghdad in the invasion. Of course, the soldiers were only jubilant after cautiously searching the building for Republican Guard as though every step could be their last and finding nothing. It was a strange pride, an ignorant pride they felt for walking in a place Iraqi government officials walked only a short time before. One of the soldiers bends down and picks up an Iraqi newspaper saying, "Look, Iraqi propaganda." It was full of articles and cartoons saying how the U.S. had invaded, with advice from the Israelis, to exploit Iraq's oil. Strange that the soldier called it propaganda. Perhaps it was true that the newspapers in Iraq were full of government propaganda. The lesson to be learned that day however, is that the difference between the Iraqi people and the American people is that when the Iraqis read the newspapers under Saddam Hussein, they <u>knew</u> they were reading government propaganda.

UNTITLED – PAUL ABERNATHY

SGT. MAJOR'S SUN PORCH

A simple whistle streaking through the air, followed by a loud
explosion, woke me from my sleep. For about the twentieth time
in country, I yelled out (or maybe it was internal) "motherfucker."
Alarm clock.

I rolled out of bed, sitting up, my head nearly missing the bunk
above me. In the darkness, my feet felt around for a yellow pair of
flip flops, shower shoes, my personal choice of foot attire. More
than likely I was in a pair of ranger panties, really short PT[1] shorts,
that were like a second skin. I slipped on an old OD[2] green T-shirt
and put on the more acceptable Army PT shorts with the liner
cut out.

People around me were yelling, but I took my sweet-ass time.
Although it was ninety degrees in the tent, it was ice compared
with the hundred-twenty outside. So, I picked up a can of dip,
my dip bottle, and flip-flopped outside. I went to the closest set
of concrete bunkers. We were sleeping in the tent just grazed by
mortars because our previous living quarters, a wooden squad bay,
had been demolished at the request of sergeant major. He wanted
a sun porch there.

So I plodded out to the bunker a few minutes later attired in PT
shorts, yellow flip-flops, green shirt, IBA[3] and helmet. Dip, water
and my M4 were in hand.

I joined the rest of the retards that signed up for this, and we all
sat, twenty of us, cramped in a five-foot-tall bunker, waiting for
the firestorm to pass. We shot the shit, talking about everything
and nothing in particular at the same time. That cramped bunker
was our universe, nothing outside, except those who would send
us out in harm's way in an attempt to track down the guys who
had just shot at us.

Within minutes, the all clear was given, meaning we should all go suit up for the bullshit mission we knew would inevitably follow. Drive out into the middle of a field, looking for people who won't be there, and search the nearest village in an attempt to feel like we're making some progress in this unwinnable situation.

...Matt Hrutkay

---

[1] Physical Training
[2] Olive Drab
[3] Interceptor Body Armor

22 October 2007

Dear Editor:

I have been assigned to spew some National Guard propaganda bullshit onto this page so you understand how awesome we are.

I am not just some citizen trying to show support. I'm an actual Guard member who has been assigned the task of writing a letter to the editor to tell you how awesome it is that we are 371 years old—more patriotic than ever!

With more politics festering in this organization than ever, I'm surprised there aren't more soldiers who have decided to speak out. The almighty hand of the president decides our next move and we follow orders. No questions asked; it's not our job to ask questions.

As each new recruit marches down the corridors of mediocrity, they don't just sign away a chunk of their lifetime; they turn in their conscience, judgment and common sense in return for a rifle and insecurity.

Do as you're told no matter how crazy it sounds. The stripes on my collar say I'm in charge and I know what's best.

I haven't seen any other business in America lining up high school graduates to sign up for a job. When it comes to dying for your country—sign here please—we provide you with job security and money for college. Just don't plan on going to college anytime soon. And I hope you realize most career fields have no use for someone who knows how to drive a tank and jump out of an airplane. Besides, now that you're in, why go to school anyway? Just retire and have nothing to show for yourself other than some colorful ribbons and the right to brag about the places you were sent.

You don't need to know why we're going here or shooting over there. The government says it knows best, so it must. They write your paycheck, anyhow. A society built on questioning the government has created the ultimate machine of unquestioning loyalty.

Not loyalty to ideals or ethics. Not loyalty to democracy or the pursuit of right over wrong, but loyalty to orders.

Brainwashed into thinking rank equals respect is just one illness bearing down on these American citizens who are among the ranks of the military. Told that their sacrifice is the ultimate show of patriotism (more times than you can count in a day), but told not to ask whether or not the manner in which you die for your country is honorable and patriotic.

If the commander in chief said it, you do it.

Why does the ultimate show of patriotism mean losing rights as a citizen? Why do new recruits need to be convinced day in and day out that they are the elite American citizens? Why do our service members have to be sold on the idea of service to country even after they've made that sacrifice?

Ultimately, why do they have to be intimidated with military laws and rules that keep them from disobeying orders based on conscience, judgment and common sense? They are stripped of these morals gradually. With more laws to keep them in the military than to help them when they're out, these patriotic citizens are given no choice but to stay.

With a contract you never read, you've been thrown into an organization where the bullies become bosses and the intelligent are looked down upon. Your education means nothing here, just your willingness to die without questions.

Sincerely,
Six Feet Under
Luke Austin

OCCUPATION – GARETT REPPENHAGEN

FBC

Earlier in my life, FBC would have always stood for First Baptist Church. That will never be true again. Fire Base Courage is more of a temple to me than any church ever has been.

I say temple because I think it fitting; it was there I prayed most often, to the hidden gods of IEDs[1] and mortars. The gods we knew were out there, choosing where and when we would once again be struck suddenly, off guard. When the thunder and concussion of an IED happened, the only bad guy I ever saw was some obscure Iraqi deity that we had pushed too far.

FBC became a church for us, using semi-religious speech when we would be surprised. Holy Shit, Jesus Christ, Oh God, were usually the first words out of my mouth when a cloud of explosive dust would instantly appear before me, behind me, or immediately outside my window.

My heart would pound, and I would get chills up my spine. This was truly a religious experience. In fact, it was such a religious experience that I am now a firm believer in the "I-don't-know-what-the-fuck-is-out-there" school of faith—much to the chagrin of my evangelical family.

But in reality, it is I who was really baptized in the fire of my new-found faith. It was a literal fire that surrounded me, more than once. Immersed in flames and shrapnel and a loud sonic boom, I felt the IED god's wrath.

Like the ancient Israelites' temple, there was a wall around the out-side, and a stone building that was the holiest of holies. This was the place where oblivious American army officers communed and tried to figure out where and when the gods' anger would release itself again. For months, we guarded this temple like the Swiss guards at the Vatican, controlling access to our place of worship.

Our bread and wine varied from day to day. Bad coffee and Red Baron pizzas were typical communion elements. The tomato sauce red like the blood of our brothers that had been shed. The coffee brown like the dirt we attempted to rinse off our bodies after we got back to Baghdad.

As time passed, we erected tents that crowded the space like the tents of nomadic worshippers. Showers and bathroom trailers were installed to make us feel human and presentable again. The brown water circling down the drain was a visible reminder of the sinful world we continually immersed ourselves in.

As in many churches, time stood still. The only evidence of change came in the changing constellations and the ticking of useless clocks. I worshipped the changing star formations, noting the change in location of the Big Dipper and Orion. I don't know why I found them peaceful and contemplative, worthy of worship. My world at the time was limited to a patch of land only a few hundred square meters large. Anything outside those walls of cinder block was alien and pagan. The hot desert sun that baked our bread, burned our offerings and heated our bodies was controlled by another god that was angry at our presence in the land of his chosen people.

The several antennae sent up prayers to the gods; signals invisible, but effectual nonetheless.

This was our temple, my church for eight months in the sand. My newfound faith in the unseen gods of destruction and uncertainty was forged in the walls of my FBC. Fire Base Courage is my newfound First Baptist Church, and in some ways, it saddens me to know that I will never worship there again.

...Matt Hrutkay

---

[1] Improvised Explosive Device

ARMY MATH — JABBAR MAGRUDER

A LETTER TO MYSELF

To Me:

Where are you going? Can you give me a hint? Did my dreams
come true (even though I didn't know what to wish for)? By now,
you have more than ten years between yourself and Iraq. But for
me, Iraq is a recently minted memory. Even with only six months
out of the Army, I still struggle to remind myself of the impact it
has had. It is hard to remember that there was another me that
existed before Iraq.

My hope is that you don't forget me like I have forgotten so many
of my predecessors. Will you let me in, be my friend? Because
I want so badly to keep these things that have happened in the
forefront of your—of my—mind.

Don't forget that it was I that rebuilt you after a year-long fire
destroyed the old foundation. I won't even begin to speculate on
all that has happened since now. But if I could see it all at the
same time, I want to be able to smile, grin, and be happy about
the things you have done.

...Matt Hrutkay

BLOOD, SWEAT AND TEARS

Blood
Squirts from the stump where the captain's hand used to be,
  before the RPG[1] hit
Blood pours from the hole in Richard's leg where shrapnel
  has invaded
Blood runs down my hands as I try to cover the wound and stop
  the bleeding
Blood and not much else are left after a car bomber hits, my friend,
Blood in my mouth as I bite my lip, praying the next mortar
  doesn't land in my fighting hole
Blood all over, once a 7-year-old boy in Baghdad discovers
  what unexploded ordinance is
Blood all over his little sister as she holds him tightly, screaming,
  and streaming down her cheeks are

Sweat
Drips down my forehead
Stinging and blinding in my eyes
Rolls off my cheek to the buttstock of my M16
Sweat covered palms shove an older Iraqi man to the dirt
Sweat covered hands zip-tie him, gag him, and place a sandbag
  over his head
Sweat falls off my chin onto him as I kick him in his chest
Sweat soaks into the handle of the axe I use to bludgeon him until
  he shuts up and stops moving and now I am covered in

Tears
Nowhere
No tears allowed in Iraq, suck it up Marine
No tears at a combat memorial service
No tears until you come home
Tears drown me as I lay in a cold bed, shaking and screaming
Blood, sweat, and tears being shed all over Iraq, all over America

The tears never stop, neither does the blood, but I don't sweat it.

...Cloy Richards

---

[1] Rocket Propelled Grenade

BLOOD, SWEAT AND TEARS PHOTOS BY CLOY RICHARDS

NIGHTWATCH – DREW CAMERON

Rifles taken from young men strapped with ammunition and given to more young men strapped with ammunition.

LIVING WITHOUT NIKKI

It didn't seem so foreign at the time, at least not until she was gone. Part of my uniform in Iraq, an essential component, was my M16A2 gas-powered magazine-fed rifle with an M203 grenade launcher. Two hundred and ten NATO[1] certified humane 5.56 mm rounds. That is seven magazines, the basic combat load. They realized that a bullet is more effective if it maims rather than kills. That the target, another human, is better neutralized if the metal stays in their body. This way, other combatants will have to tend to the wounded, a more expensive and energy-demanding situation than throwing a body in a hole. Nikki was her name. They encouraged us to develop a relationship with our rifles. Our rifle is our companion, an extension of our bodies that defines our effectiveness as a soldier, a methodically trained killer. She was always with me, always within reach. In my hands at the ready when I was on missions, one in the chamber, ready to switch from safe to semi-automatic. A few pounds of pressure on the trigger to let her speak. On my back, strapped and unloaded when walking around camp, but I always had a magazine in my pocket. Under my cot at night, nobody would touch her without my noticing. Sleeping with the strap wrapped around my arm I would nestle her against my side for extra comfort some nights. I was meticulous and thorough when I cleaned her every day. Making sure to remove all of the sand and carbon from every corner, crack, chamber and crevice. She became a part of me, a mutual relation, as I was a part of her. One of the first things I did when I returned home was give her up. They took away Nikki and locked her away. I felt lighter when I was walking around without my rifle. Sometimes a sudden panic would strike when I thought that I had left her unattended. "Oh, wait …."
We only see each other occasionally, and I sleep alone. I don't like guns anymore, but I still miss Nikki.

...Drew Cameron

---

[1] North Atlantic Treaty Organization

BOOZE ATTACK IN IRAQ

Our radio squawked out something barely audible about a vehicle approaching the convoy. My eyes scanned to my front and rear; nothing but dull green Army vehicles tearing down the highway at an amazing speed. My eyes shifted to a huge cloud of dust off the road a distance. As it approached I could make out an old, tri-colored Caprice Classic. It appeared seemingly out of midair and as it arched toward the highway, I anxiously kept an eye on it. We were on our second day of nonstop driving from Kuwait to the center of Iraq. Stories of sedans packed with Iraqis wielding AK47s and RPGs[1] attacking convoys of tanks surfaced in my head. If they are bold enough to attack tanks with Caprices, surely our "soft" convoy of cargo trucks would be a tempting target. I tightened my grip on the SAW[2] as the car reached a side road and began racing up the on-ramp of the highway. The SAW is a belt-fed automatic machine gun that looks like something Rambo would love to use. When first issued, most soldiers feel lucky to receive such a powerful and prestigious weapon. Such feelings quickly fade when you carry the damn thing around 24/7. It's heavier than an M16 rifle and you must carry a large load of ammunition.

The car leaned on worn-out shocks as it barreled through the curve. I snapped off the safety and pulled the weapon's charging handle back, chambering a round. The car continued to accelerate and merged right in the middle of our convoy on my side of the truck. Nervously I leveled the SAW at the vehicle as it drifted into the next lane. I now could see the Iraqis in the car. They were riding 6 deep and appeared to be all young men, looking as nervous and serious as me. As they came closer I could see an Iraqi in the back seat lowering the window and raising something from his lap. At the time the rules of engagement clearly stated that you must be getting shot at to return fire, or identify an armed enemy combatant. The object was thrust out of the window and I immediately recognized it. What he held was an unmistakable, dark, square bottle of Jack Daniels. In English he yelled out a price of twenty dollars. I could hardly believe it. These six guys had probably been waiting hours to ambush our convoy, not with bullets and bombs but with whisky and rum. Judging by their smiles, I don't think they realized how close I had come to turning their Caprice with worn-out shocks into a piece of scrap metal, twisted and flaming on the side of the road. Apparently they trusted the judgment of a tired and nervous 19-year-old holding a machine gun enough to approach with whisky to sell.

When no rifle barrels protruded from the windows I began to relax, and just for fun, I began haggling the price down. After several seconds of negotiations they sped up to solicit the truck in front of me. Did they really think an Army convoy, moving at top speed and stretching as far as the eye could see, would pull over to purchase whisky? We had been told the ground war would be brutal and bloody. Now only two weeks in, we sped down the main highway in southern Iraq, facing Iraqis brandishing alcohol instead of weapons. Did they think we were some type of crazed beasts coming to Iraq for a hell of a party? What had these brave entrepreneurs been told about us?

I would soon learn that there were Iraqis everywhere trying to sell booze to Americans. Not only booze but narcotics as well. Hash, downers, uppers and all types of prescription medicine could be purchased very easily wherever you found American soldiers. There was also usually quite an extensive collection of hookahs and tobacco products that could be purchased off the side of the road. Barefooted children would run along side our trucks holding tiny bags of hash in the air. They would shout "Meesta, Meesta, smoke for you Meesta!"

In situations like this, the U.S. Army trusts you with good judgment. They trust you to shoot only when necessary and to not do anything stupid. You have to learn when it's appropriate to send hundreds of burning pieces of lead at someone or when to call in an air strike. Every soldier, no matter how young or intelligent, is a link in a chain. Your responsibilities and decisions could possibly affect hundreds of lives. It has always been hard for me to understand how the U.S. Army trusts your judgment enough with a machine gun or with a million-dollar weapon system, but they won't trust you to drink a few beers in the barracks if you're underage. I still don't get it. They teach you to drive tanks, shoot howitzers and fire rockets, but no boozing if you're underage. Why, that might be dangerous!

...Nathan Lewis

---

[1] Rocket Propelled Grenade
[2] Squad Automatic Weapon

SEARCH AND RESCUE – DREW CAMERON
Two soldiers disappeared. We looked for them for three days. We found them shot dead.

WOUNDED INSURGENTS

I am usually pretty respectful when I treat wounded insurgents. They might have valuable intel, and if not, I can always use the practice. I got mad only once. I had just come off two weeks of mid-tour leave and I was still feeling refreshed from it. We had responded to a route clearance convoy that was hit by an IED.[1] The air weapons team was in the area and spotted suspected trigger men. They walked us up to them and we started to search them. The helicopters then noticed three men coming toward us attempting to ambush us 500 meters to the south. The Apaches strafed them twice with 30 mm grenades. When we maneuvered to the site, we found two men alive but in bad shape. I started to treat them when someone noticed the third man under a bush. It looked as though he took a direct hit to his lower back, his hips were mostly gone and his legs were only connected by a few strands of skin, along with other injuries. I began to apply pressure to the massive wound but it was ineffective because my hands disappeared six inches into his body. I looked at what was left of his face and it did not hide the pain he was in. I started talking to him to keep him awake but that quickly became yelling. I feel bad now; I took out my anger on him verbally as I was treating him. I was mad because it was 3 A.M. on a Friday and the mission should have ended hours ago. I was mad because if I was still home on leave I'd probably be at a party with my friends. I was mad because when I called home in a few hours, no one would understand what I just experienced. I was mad because his eyes were screaming at me. I was mad because this guy had twenty minutes left on earth and he didn't know it. I kept shutting his eyelids as I was treating him to save me from his pleading glare. I would shut them and he'd reopen them; this went on two or three times until eventually his eyes remained closed and he died. I checked his pulse to make sure and then went to help the combat lifesavers with the other patients. On the drive back I checked my watch, but couldn't read what time it was because my watch was covered in a thick coat of dried blood.

Their blood obscured my watch much in the same way that it obscured our motivations for fighting this war. Did these men hold the secrets of weapons of mass destruction? No. Were these men long lost relatives of Saddam? No. Were these men terrorist masterminds? No. These were three men in an occupied country doing what they thought was right.

...Colin Sesek

---

[1] Improvised Explosive Device

AN INTERROGATION PRIMER

You start by taking off his blindfold. You do it gently, careful not to jerk his head or neck. You untie the olive-green field dressing, filthy from the facial oils of countless other detainees. You look at him, and he looks at you, and you say, *"Salaam a'alaikum,"* and he says, *"A'alaikum salaam."* He looks young, maybe 20, tall and thin, with short hair and a short beard. He looks like any other young Iraqi—there is nothing remarkable about him. He is wearing an orange jumpsuit. You take the flex cuffs off so he can relax. Back up a few steps, now, "Smile," you say in English, and you smile at him. If he doesn't smile then you do something funny, make a funny face at him, to make him smile. Finally he either genuinely smiles or he fakes it—he's in no position to not smile for you. He must be thinking, "Why are you trying to make me smile? God knows what you are about to do to me."

You take one picture from the front and one of his left side profile. You shut the digital camera off, motion for him to sit down and have some water. The room contains one desk, three white plastic chairs, two water bottles, one pack of Miami brand cigarettes and a Rewards for Justice poster on the wall seeking information on surface-to-air missiles. You put the digital camera back in the office next door. You get a cup of coffee and the guy's file. You go back into the interrogation room. You toss the file on the desk like it is unimportant, which it is. There's absolutely nothing incriminating in it—but he doesn't know that. You tell the interpreter that he can go get a cup of coffee. He goes out of the room. You are alone with the detainee, who speaks no English. You speak very little Arabic. You ask his name. *"Shismek?"* He says Mohammed. You write it on your screening sheet. *"Mohammed aysh?"* He tells you his second name, and you write that down on your screening sheet. By this time, the interpreter is back in the room with a cup of coffee and some treats—candy or fruit, maybe even fresh dates from the kids who live on the other side of the wire who, for a dollar, will scurry barefoot up the palm trees like monkeys to get them for you. The interpreter asks if he can give some treats to the detainee. You say sure. The detainee takes the treat and places it in front of him. He seems afraid to eat it. Maybe he thinks it's poisoned.

You ask your questions through the interpreter now. It is important to always speak to the detainee directly—it builds rapport. The interpreter, though important, should remain on the sidelines. You fill out all the blanks on your screening worksheet. Name, date and place of birth, address, cohabitants, employment, military service, education level, Sunni or Shia, mosque attendance and events at the time of arrest. Name is no problem, but never forget to ask for their nickname, the *kunya*, commonly referred to as the Abu Name. Iraqis seem to know their place of birth but not when they were born, and most don't celebrate birthdays. Address— usually something like, "By the abandoned school across from the highway." Cohabitants—usually there are so many you get sick of writing and you stop the guy and just put down "None." Employment is usually day labor, meaning unemployed, only the Iraqi men are too proud to say unemployed. Military service— everyone seems to have been in Saddam's army for some time, and everyone seems to have deserted at least once. Education level can be anywhere from grade school to graduate school. Sunni or Shia? Most of the time they look at you quizzically and say, "Why are you asking *that?*" As for mosque attendance, they usually down- play it but eventually admit to at least going on Friday. Events at time of arrest are where you run into problems. That is where it gets tricky.

Sometimes you get a guy who claims to have never fired a rifle, never fired any kind of weapon at all. He says he doesn't even know what a bullet looks like, much less an RPG.[1] Sometimes you get a guy who says that he prays only on Friday, but not at the mosque. Sometimes you get a guy who says he's never been in a mosque in his life, never, never, never. Doesn't pray, drinks, smokes, womanizes. Hates Saddam, hates Muqtada al Sadr, hates Zarqawi, loves Bush. "Thank you, thank you, Mr. Bush," they all say. "Tell Mr. Bush I say thank you."

Sometimes you get a guy who all he says is *"Wa'allah, wa'allah."*
"I swear to God, I swear to God. I didn't do it." Any question you
ask him, that's what he says. Sometimes the guy just sits there and
prays out loud. You let him go on and on, and then you ask him,
what are you saying? What kind of prayers are those? And he tells
you, and you ask him about his religion and eventually he says of
course women should be stoned if they disobey you, and of course
the Shia are apostates who should be either converted to the true
path or killed. Sometimes you get a guy with the mental capacity
of a four-year-old who doesn't know the name of his village, doesn't
know how to get there, doesn't know anything, who calls Ray the
interpreter his uncle, *"Abbas, Abbas."* Sometimes you get a guy who,
when you ask him who he lives with, says in Arabic, "My Aunt has
big breasts." A guy who says that every time he sees a small child
he wants to put the child in his stomach. A guy who tries to bite
the air like a senile dog. A guy who was arrested for looking at
two helicopters flying past and counting to himself, "One, two,"
as if a highly skilled insurgent spy would need to count to two
out loud. A guy who has a scar across his forehead from a frontal
lobotomy. A blind guy, a guy with one arm, one leg. A guy with
elephantitis whose balls are the size of grapefruit. A 94-year-old
man. A 13-year-old kid.

The army field manual 34-52, *Intelligence Interrogations*, tells you
there are 17 "approaches" you can use on a person you are interrogating. Direct, Incentive, Emotional Love, Emotional Hate, Fear
Up Harsh, Fear Up Mild, Fear Down, Pride and Ego Up, Pride
and Ego Down, Futility, We Know All, File and Dossier, Establish
Your Identity, Repetition, Rapid Fire, Silent and Change of Scene.

In training, before you go somewhere like Iraq or Gitmo or
Afghanistan, the army teaches you all these approaches. Instructors
who have never performed an interrogation in the real world write
out detailed scripts where every turn and twist in the story is out-
lined, where if you don't use the Establish Your Identity approach
at a certain place in the script, you get points deducted. Then you
have training in counterintelligence investigations taught by people
who openly admit to the class that they never saw a top secret
document and never served a search warrant.

In training, it seems very clear-cut. If your detainee is a member of an oppressed minority, then you use the Emotional Hate approach to focus his hate toward the majority group that oppressed him and away from you, the American interrogator who is holding him captive. If your detainee is high-ranking and distinguished, you use the Pride and Ego Up approach to make him think he is too valuable to waste sitting in a prison camp: "Once you start working more closely with us, we can set you up with your own Iraqi National Guard Division, General."

After sixteen weeks of training and studying the manuals, you are on your own to decide questions such as: Where does Pride and Ego Down end and Fear Up Harsh begin? How do you transition from Fear Up to Emotional? What do you do if the guy starts praying out loud? What do you do if the guy fakes a heart attack? What do you do if the guy just laughs at you? Do you slap him? What if you don't slap him? Do you just let him laugh at you? Nobody in your chain of command has done this before either, so you are on your own, in "the booth" with a real, live human being who is wearing an orange jumpsuit, to whom you can do absolutely anything you want, and as long as you don't brag about it and nobody rats you out, you can get away with it.

When you leave training and come to Iraq, you bring the manuals, plans, outlines and notebooks the instructors said you would need, but you never get around to unpacking them. The manual's basic premise is that the person you are interrogating is an enemy and knows something about enemy forces. In Iraq, nobody—not your commanders, not Rumsfeld, not Cheney, not even Bush—can tell you exactly who your enemy is. You only know for sure when if they are caught with weapons or explosives—hard evidence. But those are few and far between. More common are the cab drivers, the day laborers, college professors, policemen, guys detained just for walking down the street, guys who were snitched on. You have names for these kinds of detainees. You call them dirt farmers or jaywalkers. Their offense? You refer to it as DWI—Driving While Iraqi.

There can be guidelines for interrogation, but no rules. There is no science to it. There are no scripts. There are no plans. Most often, all you know is that your guy was detained because the grunts thought he was a little suspicious—better to err on the side of caution and detain him than let the interrogators figure it out. You have five interrogations to do today, and a report to write for each one, 10 hours of work even if you half-ass it. You haven't called home in two weeks because at the end of the day you don't want to talk anymore. You would like to sleep for six hours but you know it will take you two of those hours just to fall asleep, since you can't stop imagining your own death from the nightly incoming mortar rounds. In your dreams you hear Arabic without understanding it. You have an hour with this guy to figure him out and either recommend that he go to Abu Ghraib Prison or back to his family. But you really shouldn't complain because at least you're not going out into sector everyday.

After the Abu Ghraib photos came out, the higher-ups created new strict and specific rules of engagement and standard operating procedures for the interrogators. These rules always existed, but nobody followed them, so they republished them and called them new. The rules are necessary because most of the interrogators are young, under 25 years old, with no experience in the real world, no good judgment. Good judgment is useful because it will deter you from doing things such as forming pyramids with naked detainees. The commanders and policy-makers feel uneasy about young sergeants and specialists doing interrogations. They believe they would be able to do the job better than you, but they are too busy with their other duties to even observe an interrogation, much less perform one.

You try to follow their rules, but it seems impossible at times. You would never torture people, but you know, sometimes you have to get a little rough with them, right? The rules say you cannot have any physical contact with a detainee. So, you can tell him that he will never see his infant son again because he's going to Abu Ghraib, but you can't put your arm around him when he cries?

When you show him the pictures of the hostage he is accused of beheading, and he looks away, you can't force his head to look at it? You can't slap him across the face when he gives you a cocky grin? You can't shove him against the wall? You can't kick his chair out from under him?

After a while, you create your own personal code of conduct— common sense. Common sense is crucial, because most of the people coming into the detention facility seem innocent of what they are accused of. You should be able to determine if a guy is guilty or innocent within the first half hour. If he has good evidence against him, then you go into the interrogation assuming he's guilty. If he's caught red-handed, like the guys who shot RPGs at a convoy and kept the empty launchers, then it's pretty obvious. It's hard to deny a trunk full of still-warm, empty RPG launchers. No doubt he will have a wonderful story prepared for you, and all it takes is that one unexpected question to make the story unravel. Sometimes the story just doesn't make sense, like the 18-year-old newlywed who spent four months' salary on walkie-talkies because he "just liked to play with them."

If a guy lies to you at all, you know he's guilty of something. Maybe not what he is accused of, but something. You might get a guy who is accused of being al Qaeda, or *Tawhid wal Jihad*, or of knowing Zarqawi personally—all the usual accusations. You know it's ridiculous because he's a Shiite from Sadr City, but your instinct tells you that he's hiding something. You go back and forth with him for a long time. You keep saying, "Look, I've been doing this for a while, I've interrogated hundreds of guys like you. I know you're not al Qaeda. But there's just something about you. I'm going to send you to Abu Ghraib if you don't tell me what's going on." Then he says, "I swear to God I have nothing. I love Bush." And you say, "Bullshit, I don't even love Bush, and I'm an American. In fact, I hate him. He sent me to this shithole country. Tell me what's really going on." Finally he just gets sick of the exchange and tells you he and his brother-in-law run a counterfeiting business out of their home. And you send him to Abu Ghraib anyway.

Most of the time, the only thing your instincts tell you is that the guy is innocent. A dirt farmer, a Sunni living in a Shiite neighborhood—maybe someone informed on him because he looked at someone's sister, or cut in at the gas line, or wouldn't let someone else hook into his generator. Once you find out the guy is a DWI, a dirt farmer, or a jaywalker, you treat him politely. No need to make the man an enemy. Just get the basic data for the interrogation report and figure out how to explain his innocence. Or at least write your report in such a way as to suggest *it is not reasonably feasible that the detainee is involved in anti-coalition activities.* The army doesn't teach you how to judge people's guilt or innocence in half an hour. How could they? They don't tell you how to prove someone innocent either. After all, who could've predicted that you would ever have to do that? You have to learn through experience, or not at all. You'll see that some of your fellow interrogators can't or won't learn it, so they just say every detainee is guilty, that he *showed signs of deception or became hostile during the interrogation.* Later, after you've been home six months or a year, you might wonder if it would've been better for you if you just did as they did.

You'll see that in Iraq, because of lack of personnel, many of the interrogators are arbitrarily assigned to the job. The ones put in at random are actually better than the ones who volunteer to be an interrogator, though. With the volunteers, you get the sadistic types, people who want a power trip, people with something to prove. You might see that those who don't want to be in Iraq at all, who don't even want to be in the army, are very good at interrogation. They have the ability to develop rapport with the detainees like no one else. Who better to empathize with a prisoner than one who sees himself or herself as a prisoner in the same camp? Empathy is the approach that nobody teaches you in training. How can anyone be taught to be empathetic? It is not so easy for the ordinary soldier; this is why atrocities happen.

You are surrounded by these ordinary soldiers. Most of the grunts, even some of your fellow interrogators, are just typical, ordinary soldiers. They are there to fight a war, not make friends. They want to kick ass. Most are white, Christian, from rural communities and subscribe to American values, family values. They believe in law, order and justice. Wanted: Dead or Alive. They believe Iraq has weapons of mass destruction. They sew NYPD and FDNY patches on the inside of their boonie caps. They support the president. They support the chain of command. Put yourself in the shoes of one of these ordinary, typical soldiers, and you can see how atrocities might happen:

You are away from everything you love. You wish you were back in Alabama or Texas with your young wife. You are wondering what your young wife is doing right now. You are in a shithole country, in a dirty room, sweating, sitting across from a dirty, smelly Arab in an orange jumpsuit. He has an unkempt beard and black eyes, and even though he is only 40, he seems ancient. Months later into your tour of duty, you might grow to love these people, but not right now; this is the first Arab or Muslim you have ever met. All you know about them is that they destroyed the World Trade Center. They behead people. They chant "Death to America." They danced around the wreckage of your dead friend's Humvee.

He reeks like something you have no comparison for, a smell you will identify later on in your tour as fear. You are here in this country, this situation, because of him. Your commanders told you during numerous "pep talks" that you are here to help the Iraqi people so they can have democracy and freedom, and you are protecting your own country, home and family from attack by terrorists who want to destroy the American way of life. You believe your commanders. You trust in them. You are here in Iraq because some of these assholes just won't get with the program. They don't want people to be free, they want to bring back Saddam, or to impose Islamic fundamentalism. And one of these assholes is here in the room with you, sitting across from you, and he's got a cocky look on his face. He seems proud that he's an insurgent—no, a terrorist. That's what he is, a terrorist who would kill you right now if he had the chance. Empathy, sympathy, rapport, trust, Geneva Convention—you think all that is bullshit right now, created by the liberal, politically correct politicians who never served in the military. You have buddies out there who are getting blown up every day. You need to find out who is blowing up your buddies. This is war, remember? If you were captured, they would do the same to you. No, they'd do worse. It doesn't matter how you do it. Get the information.

And that is how atrocities happen.

So, no matter how good a person you were back home, you are in Iraq now, not the United States. Good and evil are different now. Sometimes to be good you have to do things that are evil, right? You might have to lie, steal, maybe even hurt people. You might have to grab them by the neck and push them against the wall. You might have to scream at them like you've never screamed at another human being before. Or you might tell them they're going to be sent over to Egypt or Saudi Arabia, or the worst—the Iraqi Police—for questioning. "And you know, they're not going to be as friendly as I've been so far, so why don't you just answer the questions truthfully?" You sometimes might have to literally scare the shit out of them. You might have to make them urinate in their jumpsuit and then sit in it all day. Then you will have to look at the person and witness their fear and humiliation, knowing that you caused it. Will you be pleased with yourself?

More frequently, though, you will defend detainees you know are innocent, but everyone else thinks are guilty. Sometimes they might be guys who the Iraqi Police had already questioned, guys whose entire backs are just gigantic, purple bruises. Guys with two black eyes, feet covered in bruises. When you try to explain why you think these men are innocent, your commanders might say that you are a sympathizer, a "Hajji-lover." "Whose side are you on, anyway?" they might ask. Even after one of your friends gets killed by an IED,[2] they might ask you something like, "Do you think this is a joke? This is real. Our guys are getting killed every day out there."

During your tour, you might have to do a lot of things that you're not sure about. Not many of your peers will be able to give you any guidance. Many of them might come to you for guidance. What will you tell them? Do what you think is right, that's what you tell them. And for yourself, you have to tell yourself that too. Do what you think is right.

After you've been home for six months or a year, though, you might begin to wonder whether or not you did anything that was right. You might begin to think that it was all a waste. You should try to think of a few times when you did accomplish something. Remember the two truck drivers who were bringing all those 155 mm artillery rounds to the insurgents? Remember how you and Chris got them to give up their boss, Nasir? That was pretty worthwhile, right? Who knows what information Nasir gave when the other agencies interrogated him? He might have given up some other bad guys. All because the infantry guys captured two truck drivers and brought them in to you and Chris, who stayed up until four in the morning interrogating them and writing reports. That was something important that you played a little part in. That was something you did right, wasn't it?

But then you'll watch TV and you'll see that every day more kids are getting killed, most by IEDs. And you sit at home, your feet up on the coffee table, watching your digital cable while they die.

"Damn, that sucks," you might mutter to yourself as your wife sits next to you reading a magazine.

Your wife might look up from her magazine a moment, "Hm?"

"Nothing."

You feel glad that you are not over there anymore, but also a little guilty. You might still have buddies over there. You might have buddies who are already on their way back for a second tour. You may think about joining them, reenlisting. Even though you hated being there, part of you feels you belong there. You stay up late now, by yourself, going to army recruiting Web sites, or visiting the home pages of private security companies that are seeking veterans to go back to Iraq, for three times their previous salary. But then you browse the news on the Web, and you see that the latest body count is up to 2,225. General Casey is saying that we have to stay until the Iraqi Army and Police are ready to take over the job themselves—which means we'll be staying forever. After a while, you wander off to websites that show IEDs, ambushes, and beheadings, and you watch these videos on your laptop screen until your eyes are tired and you can go to sleep. You don't want your wife to know what you've been up to, so you delete the web browser's history before you shut the computer off, and then the next day she jokingly asks you, "Why did you delete the history file, hmm? Were you looking at porn?"

...Michael Nowacki

---

[1] Rocket Propelled Grenade

[2] Improvised Explosive Device

INSO-MANIA

I haven't slept in three days

I am tired

Closing my eyes does nothing for me

It gives me fear

Fear gives me rage

Rage makes my mind race

My racing mind keeps me awake

Staying awake drains my body

My drained body still produces energy

My energy makes me pace

Pacing tires my legs

My tired legs make me sit

Sitting makes my back sore

My sore back makes me lie down

Lying down makes me tired

Being tired helps me close my eyes

Closing my eyes does nothing for me

...Jon Turner

DEGRADED

there is no meaning—simple—
economy of force/d—servitude—
fangs of the beast
cry mental poison
and lose the lesser
of many evils.

---

commentary.

the bureaucratic process of our time has little meaning outside
of itself. this spiritlessness is embodied in the military doctrine
called "economy of force" (use only as much resource as minimally
possible in order to complete a mission. basically: stretch thin).
the true danger in this process is when it (inadvertently) fails or
cuts corners. it is a simple problem of bureaucracy and politics
trumping common sense.

in many cases, such conditions quickly become toxic, making men
inhuman and soldiers into war criminals. the system breeds evil,
and then the evil tree can bear little good fruit.

...Evan Knappenberger

ANXIETY OF A WEAPON MALFUNCTION

The world rattles, Kevlar hops
AKs crackle with star bursting muzzle flash
Piff, piff, pop, pop
Cover-fire!   Cover-fire!
Drop magazine, lock, load
Pop, pop, pop, snap
Cover-fire!   Cover-fire!
Shift positions, scan sectors
Snap, snap, snap
Misfire! Misfire!
Slap pull observe release tap squeeze
Slap pull observe release squeeze
Slap pull release squeeze!
Slap squeeze!
SLAP!
SLAP!
SLAP!
SLAP!

...Garett Reppenhagen

NIGHT VISION – MATT HRUTKAY

TOTAL CONTROL

New York City is terrorized
F-16s are patrolling the skies
Mobilize for world war, no questions asked
There is no future when you've erased the past

History rewritten to cover up our lies
The Pentagon's watching—you'd better close your eyes
NSA's surveilling every thought of dissent
My friend's been disappeared—they won't say where
he's been sent

Tell us the truth—why'd you send us to Iraq?
Your hands stained bloody red, and petrodollar black
You speak of human rights, you speak of liberty
But you've sold the cartels shares of foreign policy

Refineries run on the blood of U.S. troops
Reconstruction managed by criminals in suits
Paying trafficked workers a colonial wage
And no one takes a stand 'til it hits the front page

Energy market hit list in a neverending war
It's no secret who and what we're fighting for
Addicted to power, controlled by fear
When the goal is total control, it's clear the end is near

...Thomas Buonomo

Women wailing
All in black
Such an outpouring of grief
Vocal, Physical, collective mourning
When did we forget to mourn?
As a country, as individuals
Where is my grief,
What do I mourn for?
Rarely it comes, but it comes in waves
Sobbing for what has been lost
For all of us, for humanity,
For that old man throwing himself
on the ground over & over, & over,
Screaming + grabbing his head
The loss surrounds us forever
As it always was + always will be

FUNERAL — KELLY DOUGHERTY

THE MEK — DREW CAMERON
Mujahadin el-Khalq, an Iranian dissident group living in eastern Iraq. We took an array of weapons; this time, surface rockets.

UNTITLED

A skirmisher hole is a hasty fighting hole to the military;
to me it's a shallow grave.

That is what they made me dig,
in this place so far away from home.

My own grave to die in,
and be forgotten about.

How many flags will they wave in my memory,
how many more meaningless stickers will they sell?

I'm going to die alone,
in a grave I dug for myself.

...Bryan Casler

THE WALK

It was a May day like any other as we pulled into the poorly forti-fied Traffic Police Headquarters compound. We parked in our usual spots and the squad leader rallied us around him. He had a BOLO (be on the lookout) list in his hand, and we were to check license plates in the adjacent parking lot against it. He needed about half the squad; I was one of them.

It was about a one hundred meter walk between the parking lot and our location in north Baghdad. In our way was a small market, a crowded small market, and we made our way toward it. As we fanned out, I saw all the blustering and posturing my comrades were doing; they looked ridiculous. They were wearing body armor, helmets, sunglasses, pistols, and semi-automatic assault rifles; they didn't need to intimidate anyone with their behavior. As we approached the market, I saw the Iraqis' faces; they looked apprehensive. What was going on? What was going to happen? Why do they look so angry?

"Sergeant Jackson, can I fuck with somebody? Please, let me fuck with somebody!" one of our junior NCOs[1] asked our squad leader.

The squad leader said that it might not be a good idea to piss anyone off, especially when we were outnumbered and had to come here practically every day for the next nine months—never mind that it was just plain wrong. Wrong was not something that the young sergeant would have responded to however, so I don't fault the man for omitting the most obvious argument against the request.

We continued walking toward the market, and I could now make eye contact with the people there: the passersby; the shopkeepers; the shoppers; the old men drinking chai under a canopy … all of them. They looked frightened. They looked angry. They looked hopeless. I made eye contact; I smiled. *"Salaam a'alaikum,"* I said in my poor Oklahoma-dialect Arabic. Some smiled back and replied *"Alaikum a'salaam"* in the same nervous manner that I had greeted them; others continued to stare. Activity slowed all around us; we were the center of attention.

"Hey, Sergeant Stephens; that guy's staring at you!" one said with a laugh and a smile.

"I'll kick his fucking ass!" Stephens yelled with an exaggerated arch of his back and raise of his shoulders. Now, everyone was staring and the looks of despair and hopelessness deepened. What could anyone do? What could the man in question do? We were armed to the nines and wrapped in body armor; the staring man was in a tunic and sandals.

… and why wouldn't he or anyone else stare? They tolerated us at the police stations and on the roads, but this was their territory. Why were we there? This was out of the ordinary, and they had every right to wonder, every right to stare. They were scared, worried, angry.

As we made our way into the market and started splitting up to search the parking lot, two old men sat at a table to my left. They were old; they looked wise. They both stared at me like they would at a disappointing adult grandson: saddened, disappointed, resigned to my and their respective fates. They weren't angry; they were just sad. There was a lot of wisdom in the creases that stretched out from their old, tired brown eyes. They had probably seen more war than I ever will, and they were tired. I gave a nervous smile, an embarrassed smile, and made my way into the parking lot.

As I looked out over the vast parking lot, the sheer lunacy of this mission hit me. Here we were, looking for ten cars in a city of five million people. It was unlikely that we'd find one of them, but it was highly likely that we had just alienated a few more Iraqis. At that moment I empathized with the Iraqis still staring at me from the market. I felt hopeless, saddened, disappointed, just a tad angry and resigned to my fate: I would spend the next eight to nine months performing counterproductive missions like this one. At the end of every day, I would make a few more enemies than I killed or brought to our side. I was embarrassed and humiliated that I ever thought differently; I wanted to tell the people behind me that I was sorry for what my country had done for the past three years. I was sorry we had interrupted their mundane commerce that day in the market.

Like a good soldier, I drove on. I continued to search; I continued to do my job, just as I would the rest of my tour. In front of me, two men were trying to push-start an old rickety van. I had thought of helping them, but I was carrying the M249 SAW machine gun with no sling; there was no way I was going to set it down or ask someone to hold it so I could help. Then I heard Sgt. Stephens' muffled voice. *"Fuck it; we're supposed to be winning hearts and minds, right?"* Stephens sighed under his breath. I watched, shocked, as the same man who had just lobbied to *"fuck with somebody"* slung his rifle and helped these men get that van started as I covered him from a safe distance. It was indicative of his seemingly bipolar personality, I thought as we all met up in the rear of the parking lot.

"Any luck?"

There wasn't any, and we made our back through the parking lot, to the market, through the market, to our Humvees in the police station. As I passed through the parking lot that last time, the same old men stared at me once more. Our eyes met again, and I nodded in their direction. They nodded back, and I felt like I was forgiven.

I made it back to my Humvee, sweaty and slightly out of breath, and didn't think about those old, tired men again for quite some time. It wasn't until August that the thought of those grandfatherly figures again crossed my mind.

It was August and it was hot. We were running late, and, as we approached the police station, we saw a familiar plume of smoke: car bomb. We parked as usual; SSG Jackson asked me to monitor the radio and provide security while he and others went to investigate.

I wanted to protest; I wanted to go. I wanted to check on Ali and Achmed, my Iraqi friends. I didn't see them as I normally did as we pulled into the station, and they could have been in the carnage. Those boys were what had kept me sane for the previous eight months, and I was worried about them. But I didn't protest; I did what I was told.

When the men returned, they told me of the death and destruction they had just seen and I was slightly glad I didn't witness it.

"Man, two old men were just sitting there drinking chai and it went off next to them; they're fucked up!" One soldier said, clearly not joking and certainly not making light of it.

… and there it was. The eyes that had told me how hopeless and resigned to their fate the men were, the eyes that had forgiven me, were dead, never to pass on any of their wisdom again. I felt sad; I felt like the world had just lost a couple of good men, even though we never spoke.

I started to remember all the faces I saw during The Walk, all the eyes I looked into. How many were gone? How many had forgiven me and my country? How many would die before I left? It was unsettling, but it was by now not at all uncommon. I was tired, physically, but mostly emotionally. Mentally, I just gave up, and, as I hoped I would see Ali and Achmed soon, I slid deeper into my body armor and took a nap while my comrade monitored the radio.

...Justin Cliburn

---

[1] Non-Commissioned Officers

CARETAKER — KELLY DOUGHERTY

RAMĀDĪ

RAMADI – AARON HUGHES

SHACKLED

Shackled by my grief

The letters seared into my flesh

This pain is for Tim

These tears are for him

He was my little brother

He died in Iraq last Saturday

...Mike Blake

BLAKE — DREW CAMERON

The following is a version of the letter sent to Seven Days, a local Burlington newspaper, that was published on October 24, 2007.

To the editor of Seven Days, or to whomever else this concerns, I am writing on behalf of myself as well as other fellow Iraq Veterans Against the War. I would like to respond to Judith Levine's comments in the article "Honor Guard" published last week. First off, my name is Jon Turner. In August, I departed the main gates of Marine Corps Base Camp Lejeune for the last time. I have been on three deployments, two of which were in Iraq where I served as an infantryman. As an infantryman I was responsible for kicking in the doors of innocent Iraqi families and occupying their homes at the early hours of the morning and late hours of the night. During my tours in Iraq I have witnessed and been a part of disrespectful acts toward innocent civilians and detainees. Yes, at the time we laughed, but due to what I have experienced and witnessed, I now have post-traumatic stress disorder. I'm sorry, but I do not consider this a disorder. Due to my actions that I willingly did, it is my fault that I have flashbacks of mortar rounds, snaps of machine gun fire coming past my head and other large explosions and loud noises. Let's not forget the dead bodies, some of which I created, and our fellow brothers and sisters who have died. I volunteered for Marine Corps Infantry because I thought I was going to fight a "proper" fight. Reality has shown that is not what is happening. I did not sign up to see innocent people get hurt and die. I did not sign up to identify my dead friend Richard Zachary James after he had just been shot by a foreign sniper right at the top of his forehead. Yes, I signed the contract, but myself as well as many other war veterans also figured we would get help for the physical and psychological problems that are a direct result of going to war, regardless of whether the war we are fighting in is justified or not. Levine says support the troops as humans, but do not support the troops for what goes on in war. Well, those who have been to war— especially those who have walked the streets and been shot at or blown up—will tell you that your mind goes to a different place in war. If you want to support the troops, help them when they get home and listen to them when they speak. My apologies for not getting this in sooner. I was at the Different Drummer, a GI coffee shop in Watertown, NY, at a workshop with other members of Iraq Veterans Against the War working on our writings and poetry, which will be put into a book called Warrior Writers. Thank you for listening.

Jon Turner
Burlington, VT
Iraq Veterans Against the War

FOOD, WATER & REVOLUTION

Katrina didn't burst the levees
I think it was the system we live in
I call it capitalism
They put blacks and Latinos in prisons
and send the poor to Iraq
Now there's not enough troops
for the state to call back
Bodies are floatin'
but not enough are revolting

The stench of dead children
smell like the streets of Baghdad
Corpses stacked in the streets
zipped up in black bags
The black gold of the Middle East
lets you capitalists thrive
while poor blacks in New Orleans
rot in the streets and die

You sent troops to free Iraqis
from the blood in their veins
You sent troops to liberate
Afghan skulls from their brains
You sent troops to bring peace to Fallujah
with your jet bomber planes
And troops can't stop a hurricane
but the deaths are insane
You sent us to New Orleans
but you waited four days

We marched through the streets
and we received our orders
When threatened shoot to kill
but we saw the horrors

Stank toilets overflowing
No running water
Women givin' birth to kids
in dark hospital corners

You apologists for the bosses
claim the wreckage was nature
But your scientists knew
the levees would fail us
You could have rebuilt marshes
had fifty years to maintain 'em
But you turned your back on the poor
and you still claim you're making us safer
You don't care about workers
you care about making the paper

We make everything
you control our wealth
You turn *our* labor into *your* profits
forsake our safety and health
not that *your* dollars
would ever go to ourselves
You poured billions into Bourbon St.
Stadium, ports and pumping oil wells
You don't care if the poor drown
floating in their shacks
Just another genocide
like you're doing in Iraq
and like you did
with the slaves
Over 1 million drowned
in watery graves

Now we're in a war
where you protect us from terror?
United We Stand
like we're all in this together

Just trust in the government
Do what you say
thousands drowned with no relief
survivors rotted away
You militarized streets
to protect empty stores
Instead of rescue, water, food
You spend money on wars

I've come to realize
I should expect nothing less
Katrina wasn't a mistake
just capitalism at its best

Some might wonder
why I criticize the U.S.
But everywhere I look
capitalism caused this mess
Under this system workers get no relief
You pit our class against ourselves
women and workers of color
You recruit us into armies
to fight our sisters and brothers
You fund political Islamists
create suicide bombers
give birth to terrorists like
Osama, Saddam, and Congress

You say fight for your country
to serve and protect
but we just serve you and your banks
You collect the checks
We collect the dead

You order me to kill for your business
But I refuse
and I'm not the only one
Katrina lit the fuse

We've multiplied and organized
and we're planning your doom
there's two classes and one Earth
that's just not enough room

Every worker that survived
can see the ways of your system
Elderly, babies dying
from no air conditioning
Not enough are ready to fight
But tens of millions are listening

And what would've happened
if we would have seized their buses
Led every poor person to safety
if troops refused orders, said, "Fuck this.
We ain't killing poor people just like us."
Blasted off the bosses
turned their dollars to dust
if every worker at the Superdome
picked up planks, knives and chromes
Raising the flag screaming
the Red Cross ain't our solution
we need food, water and revolution

...Fernando and Maria Braga

FUEL LINE — KELLY DOUGHERTY

A SANDSTORM — A DUSTSTORM —
BLOWN TO
SEA COATS YOUR
VESSEL WITH
A CAKING OF
GEORGIA RED CLAY
THAT CAN BE
BLOWN AWAY WITH
FIRE HOSES, BUT
IS NOT GOOD for THE
AIR INTAKE & Systems
for THE DIESELS or for
THE AIR INTAKE Systems of
the peoples with grit
in their teeth and mud in
their lungs.

*AND MILDEW
GROWS ON
THE P.F.D.² IN
THE ABANDON
SHIP LOCKER
AND LOOKS
LIKE THIS

DO you see How the water sloshes
BACK AND forth in the Northern Arabian Gulf?
It MAKES CHOPPY WAVES MORE
Reminiscient of LAKE Huron's than of
Any tropical SEA I've Known.

A TRIP TO THE ZOO

So BIAP[1]
Been here a few times with nothing to show
Been stopping here for chow and showers and sleep
Sleep on my cab, warm and oily dust covered cab
Sleep
That's all I want to do in the black generator roaring motor pool
Get a picture of this sign
Get a picture in the morning in this safe zone with Kevlar off
    and flack vest off
Hey mom, dad, this is BIAP
Your son is in BIAP with his shit truck
Hauling a shit Humvee burnt and brown and crumbling
    back to Kuwait

BIAP — AARON HUGHES

But I'm here Mom Dad Stepmom Stepdad Sister Brother
What the fuck am I here for?
Was it the generators, bunker busters, busted conexes,
Safe in BIAP
Holy ground of miles of airplanes and lies

...Aaron Hughes

---

[1] Baghdad International Airport

MACHINE, MECHANISM ... PARTS

I am a hero if I kill other men. I am a coward if my conscience keeps me from killing other men. What sordid brutal excuse of a world is it that we live in when this WARPED version of reality is acceptable?

The machine runs with the sole purpose of inflicting destruction, death, racism and false authority. And when one mechanical part of the machine ceases to operate properly (as with myself), the machine does not care about the human value of that mechanical part (me). Nor does it care what human reason caused the part (me) to fail to operate any longer and contribute to the machine. I am that mechanical part, not a human. Bottom line ... that's all the Army has is a bottom line. There is no value for life in the Army. No one is equal. No one is free. No one has the right to think for themselves. Iraqi civilians are not people. They do not work to provide nourishment for their families like Americans. And when they strap a bomb to their chest or set off an IED[1] they are terrorists, not humans that are defending their homeland to a brutal occupation force. Hajjis, camel-jockeys, towel-heads and sand niggers—that's all they are; these names are used to measure their worth, to dehumanize.

The machine convinces me that I will shoot at them, kill them and then laugh at them as I walk past their mutilated corpse. Then there's the award ceremony, medals for killing. I return home a ... hero? This machine ... is nothing more than glorified organized crime. They used me, used me as a mechanism to contribute to a selfish machine of incomprehensible malice. I am not a mechanism ... parts. I am taking back those parts, all of them, the parts of my soul that contributed to the machine. I am leaving the family never to return. I have had enough of organized crime. Recovery and self-discovery are what I face. But slowly, steadily and hopefully I will be whole again. I will take back who I am at my core—a human being with a soul—and I will stop acting for and thinking like the machine.

...Jared Hood

---

[1] Improvised Explosive Device

CONVOYED — DREW CAMERON

SHE IS NOT BLOWING KISSES, SHE IS BEGGING FOR FOOD — AARON HUGHES

MENTAL IMAGE

There are images that people can easily see. Photographs and videos are the most common ways people can see Iraq. The problem is that it's just an image. It lacks the actual scars that are left on the people that saw the event firsthand. There are emotions behind images. There are sights and smells that will never leave an individual's mind. When all the scenes are put together with an image, the real truth comes out of it. It can be seen as a whole, not a piece of paper with colors and shapes.

there is this ball of fire that is constantly on my mind
one that sneaks up on me any hour of the day
an enormous explosion that ended the lives of two marines

There are no photographs of this event. Instead, there are mental images that my platoon and I will hold onto forever.

...Evan Moodie

[THIS PAGE LEFT INTENTIONALLY BLANK]

GIT

Lose me, allow me to die
Although I am forgotten by history
Posterity will judge us
As we are now

Force me to defeat myself
No one is watching
I will not be missed
As I stand now

Flagellate me, sneer at me
Your jests do not fall
On idle ears
Nor will they always

Forget me, let me fail
And all will be lost
Destroy what makes a man
And you will destroy that man

...Evan Knappenberger

WHAT DID I DO IN THE WAR?

The year 2003 was pivotal in my life. Though I had been to the Gulf region before for combat, it was my first time as a soldier. Before I had been younger and in the Navy. Leaving was somewhat easier back then, but now the pain of little girls pleading me not to go was the most horrific battle I had ever faced. I dealt with the internal struggle by telling myself that someone had to do it. After all, I was one of Ronald Reagan's cold warriors, born and bred to defend democracy.

After weeks of endless missions in Iraq, the anticipated news that weapons of mass destruction had been found and that our efforts to save the world were fruitful never came. When the invasion was complete and the mission changed to flying loads of charcoal and nearbeer and picking up the occasional officer and staff, the lull made morale hard to keep up. Even with our limited news from the outside, the question "Why are we still here?" was not answered. I began to question my worth.

The dark cloud of futility was nearly overwhelming. I finally found a productive way to feel a sense of worth. In every tent entrance were stacked boxes sent by a supportive American public. These care packages were filled with items for the troops. Many were being thrown away. As I flew over the Iraqi people's dwellings I found my idea. Though I know in other conflicts many others have done this before, it was time for the return of the candy bomber. Each day I would fill PX[1] bags with treats, hygiene items and toys, whatever I could get my hands on, and drop them over tents and houses along our route. My pilots and fellow flight engineers enjoyed it as it helped break the monotony of our long missions. The challenge: to release the bags close to, but not on, the homes. Soon soldiers began dropping off bags and donations at my tent. The operation expanded. Other crews would ask me for a "bomb load" for their mission.

On my last mission in Iraq, to an outpost known then as Edson, I was making my drops on the way out. From my gun position on the aircraft ramp, I slung the bag out and almost immediately felt a huge blow to my chest, knocking the wind out of me. As the area of Edson was hostile, we were always alert for ground fire. The possibility of getting hit was always there. My immediate thought was how sorry I was for the pain that I would cause my girls. I told myself, "Wow, you really don't feel the one that gets you." When I reached for my mic cord to tell my fellow crewman that I thought I was hit, I saw part of a plastic PX bag flapping from inside my vest. I started laughing and shared one at my expense with the rest of the crew. The candy bomb (about five pounds) had caught the CH-47 rotor wash, and shot back in and struck me in the chest. A few clicks more and I released it near the next tent.

I had spoken with a chaplain at one of our many stops, who told me the orphanages in Iraq made the children fund's info-mercials look like resorts, so all 700 pounds of donations I had left I delivered to him as we ceased missions and headed home.

This is the story I tell when I am asked, "What did you do?" In light of the truth about our occupation of Iraq, maybe it was all that I accomplished. I came back changed. No more blind trust in the politicians to wield our forces offensively, and a profound sense of caring for all people we share this planet with.

...Chris Ritter

---

[1] Post Exchange

PASSION'S HEARTS

"All that sadness just lingers.
It just hovers there."
He goes in first and is not afraid.
He's been here before but not me.
Some trees stand and some still fall.
The courtyard of this public garden is empty today
Save for us.
And now only me since my brave has gone into the surgery place.
Now holds only coddling figs and abandoned art and me.
Standing in a mine field of botanical hearts
Strewn 'round about my wary feet
And I know not to move
And I do not move
But stare at a thousand Iraqi flies

Traveled all this way to feed on passion's hearts and realize my fears.
And I will not move from fear, for fear
And I do not want to see what I know I am about to see.
The flies' black cloud rises as the marine welder surgeon
Emerges from the cave with the dead man in his arms
Or half of him
And I am even less prepared than I thought.
Deep inside my gut the echo rips through
Of that sixteen-year-old explosion
That took the life of the thing
And sucked the air from the air
And nothing yet has returned to grow.
Please don't make me look.
And God said, "Look at my beautiful child."

PASSION'S HEARTS PHOTOS BY MARCUS ERIKSEN

Now it's left to me to bring the rest
And I will
For love of the brave and for my own healing too
Or not.
The legs, permanently cocked and appropriately supine

But for these four minutes
Of pall-bearing these ball bearings
And four legs is not enough for running me far enough away
From where I've never been.
I've known the silent or at least quiet reverence appropriate
  to the dead
And I practice it now
No less than if metal were meat.
It is right that I should do so
And I do
Even though doing what is right is at the very bottom
  of my list right now
And yes, that is a lie
But if wishing it wasn't would make it true,
God and Satan's gospel it would be.
I'll sit for an impromptu eulogy
And let but not make feeling.
All is quiet
All is reverent
Mature sadness and not contrived.
We join the other congregants for daily procession into the sun
All come together at last where drivers are wanted.
Inside our rented hearse
We are three brothers.
One sings.
One cries.
One is silent.
Which does which I'll let you decide.

...Jeff Key

142

WINDSHIELD – MATT HRUTKAY

TEARS IN BAGHDAD

It never ends.

Ali was trying to tell me something about Achmed with a serious-
ness I had yet to see from him, and I took it to mean that Achmed
had somehow been injured in an explosion, but I wasn't sure. With
the language barrier, it was difficult to understand what was being
said all the time, even with the seemingly obvious body language.
These boys had been regular fixtures in my life, sharing laughs
and smiles, but we by no means always knew what was being com-
municated. One time, I thought that Achmed was telling me
Ali had been hurt in a blast, but it turned out he was saying that
Ali was working on his home, so this could have been anything.
I told myself it was probably nothing and tried to forget about it;
ignorance is bliss.

I thought about what it was that Ali was trying to tell me all weekend. Ali and Achmed were my saving grace in Iraq: those boys had
been what had kept me sane for the last nine months. They couldn't
have been more than fourteen years old, but they had seen more
than I ever will. Their sense of humor and positive attitudes were
infectious, however, and I and the rest of my squad had unofficially
adopted them months before. Baghdad seemed a lot more like home
with those kids around.

I wish I was right about it being nothing; I wish that Achmed was
simply working on his house. After a few days of walking around
in denial, I again saw Ali and this time I had our linguist mediate
the conversation. According to Ali, Achmed and his mother had
gone to the fuel station to buy fuel for their home. As they were
leaving, a suicide bomber appeared and Achmed, who was holding the
can of fuel, and his mother were engulfed in a ball of fire. Achmed's
mother had died instantly. Achmed was burned terribly from head
to toe. As he sat in an Iraqi hospital, his father was out doing
anything he could to come up with the money for his treatment,

as there is no insurance and hospitals there expect payment up front. I felt like I had just lost a lifelong friend, if not a family member. For all I had done for those two young men, I felt so helpless that no matter what I did in our trivial hours together at that police station, I would never be able to protect them from the horrors of everyday life in Baghdad. When I left them each day, I returned to the heavily fortified base complex that allowed me to sleep easy at night. Of course, it was hard to rest easily when you know that your friend is in horrific pain in a substandard hospital, and the bags under my eyes could attest to how worried and tired I had become. Two other guys and I did what any self-respecting men would do: we gave what little cash we had to help pay for our friend's hospital bill. Together, though, we were only able to give him roughly $30. If there had been an ATM nearby, I would have contributed my daily limit to that poor boy's hospital care, but life in Baghdad limits you in ways that you never know until they appear.

What upset me was the general indifference the rest of the squad treated the news. Some gave an unconvincing exclamation of their sorrow, but all said they had no money ... something that I know was untrue. Some cited their inability to believe Ali 100% for their reluctance to help, but I found that to be nothing more than a cop-out. Say, for example, that Ali made it all up, and he and Achmed were splitting the proceeds behind our backs; what are you out? $5? $10? Weigh the risk and reward of that scenario in your head: if you are right, you have thus gained a whole $10; if you are wrong, an innocent little boy waits in pain as his father searches for a way to pay for his treatment. Take into account the risk of infection and the prompt treatment of his injuries becomes imperative. What further blew their argument out of the water was that these were not exactly fiscal conservatives we are talking about. They blew money on two or three DVDs a week (at almost $20 a pop), ate Pizza Hut, Popeye's, Burger King, and Hardee's at least four times a week; paid crazy amounts of money for fancy coffee in the morning from Green Beans Coffee (usually $5 a cup); the list goes on.

These, aside from two individuals, were also the religious wing of the squad. They had told me that they are Christians and wish to live a Christian lifestyle, and they had questioned my lack of faith. No amount of religious posturing, however, will make me forget how they elected to treat not only our friends Ali and Achmed, but the Iraqi people in general. If any one of them ever again in my lifetime attempts to tell me what Christianity is about or what they are about, I will not hesitate to throw this back in their collective faces. This is just one example of their hypocrisy, but I think it is the most glaring. Good Samaritans they were not. This is not to criticize the faith itself, but I never again want to hear these men pretend to be men of God.

All I could do over the weekend was hope that the money raised was enough to precipitate the treatment of Achmed and that that treatment could have at least alleviated the pain he was in. I had said many times before that I will never forget about these young men, and that hasn't changed. I am so thankful that my children, when I have children, will not be subjected to the things these boys were.

That night, an Iraqi girl instant messaged me out of the blue. She was worried that I might be reluctant to speak to an Iraqi woman, but I assured her that was not a problem. We talked online for hours about our respective lives and how different and alike they were. It wasn't long before she asked me about my Yahoo picture, which was one of little Ali wearing my helmet and goggles. I told her about him and Achmed, what I had done with them and the bond we had forged. I expressed my regret that I had not been able to do more for them, and she really put me at ease. She said, "I think you have done all you could have done and I think you are a very kind man …. They will never forget you, you know." A peace truly did come over me after hearing that; perhaps I needed to hear it before I left my habibis, my good friends. It made the day's news just a little more bearable and alleviated any guilt I may have been feeling.

If I were a man of faith, I would have been convinced that she was an angel, because no one on this Earth could have made me feel as at peace as she did in that moment. Somehow, she picked the perfect time to come into my life and I thank her to this day for that.

I spent that weekend hoping against hope that Achmed would be okay. I had hoped that our money was enough to get him the treatment he needed, that he received it in time, that he had not succumbed to infection, and that he was in as little pain as humanly possible. Within minutes of arriving at the police station, I saw Ali and knew that I would have some type of news. As I approached him, his eyes met mine, and I knew. As Ali made a digging motion towards the ground and repeated "Achmed, Achmed" over and over, the cold reality sunk in: Achmed was dead.

Ali said that Achmed's father had told him to please thank us for all we had done for him and especially for the money we gave him to pay the hospital. Ali thanked us profusely for trying. Of course, I didn't think we did anything incredibly special. Achmed was a friend and a friend in need. I did what friends do; I helped as much as I could.

After sharing the terrible news with me, Ali begged me once again for a picture of me, him, and his best friend, and this time I couldn't drag my feet. I knew that I had to get those pictures developed and in his hands as soon as possible. In the meantime, he said he wanted a picture of me and my family and I obliged. I took out a photo of our family portrait and wrote "To my friend Ali, Justin" on the back. He was happy and said that he would try and get a picture of Achmed with his family for me.

The news was sobering and not at all what I was hoping to hear, but the memory of the day is bittersweet. Sergeant Bruesch and I talked to Ali for at least a couple of hours and we all shared nervous laughs. Later, Gonzo, our linguist, came out and translated every-thing. He said that Achmed had given him the shoes I bought for him, but they were too small. I told him I would bring him a bigger pair the next week, and we shared a smile and a firm hand-shake (Ali never hugged and gave cheek-kisses like Achmed) as he left us to go collect some more cans.

The last time I had visited with Achmed, I taught him how to play "Rock, Paper, Scissors" and laughed as he went "rock" twenty hands in a row. We goofed off playing for twenty minutes, and I'll never forget him giggling like the little boy he was as I tried to explain something to him that he obviously didn't understand, as long as it was in English. No matter; we killed a lot of time and had some fun doing it. He again asked me over and over when I was going to give him a picture of him, Ali, and me together, and I told him I would get it to him before I left. Oh, how I wish I had gotten it to him in time, but I always thought I'd have time later. When it was time for me to leave, he gave me two kisses on the cheek and told me he would see me next week. That was the last memory I will have of him, and it is a cherished one.

I know that I meant a lot to him, or at least brightened a number of his days. I know I did, but I don't think he ever knew how much he had meant to me. He and Ali were what I looked forward to on mission days. On weekends, I thought about them. I dreamt I had adopted them. They brightened my day as much as I did theirs, and I worried about them when I didn't see them. Every time there was an attack or an explosion in that area, I held my breath until I saw them again. I knew that this day may come, and I wasn't particularly surprised or angry when I heard the news. I accepted it rather matter of factly, but I indeed hurt inside. Afterwards, I sat in my Humvee silently as tears rolled down my face. I didn't sniffle. I didn't wail or moan. I didn't punch anything. I didn't even breathe heavily, but I cried. It was a type of cry that I had never before ex-perienced. I felt like I was watching myself deal with the news from someone else's point of view; I felt detached.

How had this happened? What did Achmed do? All he was guilty of was being born in Baghdad. He was a victim of circumstance, bad luck, bad timing, and, some would say, fate. He did what millions of people do everyday: he bought fuel from the neighborhood fuel station. At that same time, someone detonated a suicide vest and Achmed and his mother were lost.

As I went from tears and sullen silence to bittersweet reflection and drier eyes, I took out my journal (which I had not written in nearly as much as I should have) and started writing what I was experiencing. At that time, the cutest little girl, maybe three years old, passed by holding the hand of her father. I couldn't help but wonder how long she'd be allowed to live, how long she'd be allowed to be a child. I certainly hope it is longer than Ali and Achmed got. She looked so much like my brother's daughter; it was uncanny. I was immediately grateful that my niece was being raised in the United States, far from IEDs,[1] car bombs, and mortars. It is unfair indeed, and it is easy to feel a certain level of guilt. I know, however, that I had about as much control over where I was raised as Achmed did. It's no one's fault, and there is no sense in feeling guilty over it. I took solace in what Sarah (who lived in Baghdad) had told me about these two boys in our instant message conversation the night I had first heard the news about Achmed. She was certain that I had done everything within my power to help the young man, and I had made a difference in his life that I could never measure. That comforted me.

I was also slightly comforted in knowing that he was no longer suffering. Third-degree burns can be extremely painful, even with the world's best medical treatment; they must have been terrible in an Iraqi hospital with limited resources. I did not want to think of what pain he felt in his last few days; I was just thankful that it was over. If I had to pick one memory of him, it would be the sight of his face peering into the Humvee window looking for me, and then his yell of "Justin!" when he spotted my face. I will surely remember that face for the rest of my life; I had never seen anyone, outside of my parents, so happy to see me.

Two weeks had gone by since I learned of Achmed's death and had promised Ali a picture of the three of us together. My mom did a great job of developing the pictures I sent her and shipping them back in a folder for Ali. I was ready to fulfill my promise.

Within minutes of arriving at the Traffic Police station, I heard the familiar voice yell my name; it was Ali. I walked over to him calmly, shook his hand, and simply said, "Pictures." "Achmed!?!" he asked excitedly. "Yes." As I turned around to go retrieve the pictures, I heard Ali behind me telling one of my comrades in his broken English that I had pictures of Achmed for him; it dawned on me just how important this was to him.

I brought the folder to him and recognized a familiar look on his face, yet it had been years since I had seen that look. It was the face of a boy at Christmas waiting for the go-ahead to rip open his presents. The folder had barely switched hands before he had pulled it out of its envelope and opened it to page one. Staring back at him was a full page picture of Achmed, smiling like always. I saw a sudden shift in Ali's posture, and he slowly fell to his knees … and wept. He tried to hide his face, hide his sniffles, hide his breathing, but it was to no avail. Ali wept like a little boy, and I had never heard a little boy weep for such a just reason. These were tears of love, friendship, memory, and closure. I'd seen those tears before, but rarely had they come from the eyes of a boy so young, yet so aged. Such is life in Baghdad.

I tried to comfort him; I did what I could. I placed my hand on his back and told him it was okay. He was embarrassed, but no one could fault him for letting it all go. As I uneasily watched him alternately weep, look at the photograph again, and wipe his eyes, a strange peace came over me, and it was then that I realized it: this was my closure. I had fulfilled my promise to Ali and, post-humously, Achmed to bring them pictures of the three of us together—we, the "Three Habibis." I didn't get to witness a funeral, or a eulogy, or wake, or burial, or memorial, but I got to see the emotions that were present in all five. Ali was certainly solemn and depressed when he first told us of the news, but other than the deep sorrow I saw in his eyes, I saw very little emotion. If the tables were turned, I would have expected to see Achmed cry every day; he was a very emotional kid, but Ali had always been a little bit more reserved. Ali tried to be a tough guy; Achmed just acted like a kid.

Ali was embarrassed and composed himself within a couple of minutes, but he cried just long enough for him to get it out of his system and for me to feel like a chapter in my life was indeed coming to a close. He cheered up and was back to his usual self again. I gave him some socks that he had asked for the previous week and he told us that someone had tried to steal his "junta" (backpack) after he left us last time, but he had thrown "chocolata" in the opposite direction for them to chase while he ran away. We all shared a laugh and were in mutual agreement that the awkward moment of before was over, though no one said it outright.

Before he left, he said, in one way or another, several times that it will be a sad day for him when I returned to the States and indicated that tears may flow by repeating a wiping motion across his eyes. He asked me if America would be good for me without Ali, and he asked how much time I had before I left him. Guilt is not the correct word, but I was sure I would feel something when I left and it wouldn't dissipate simply because I was home and away from the tears in Baghdad. I knew that I would be leaving one of my best friends, and I didn't like it, but I knew I would have little choice in the matter.

That day has come and gone, and I still think of my Iraqi friends and those tears in Baghdad. Not a day goes by that I don't wonder how Ali is doing or how Achmed's father is coping with the loss of his wife and son. I left Baghdad eight months ago, but Baghdad has yet to leave me. I don't think it ever will … and I don't ever want it to.

...Justin Cliburn

---

[1] Improvised Explosive Device

I AM WHO SURVIVED FORGIVE ME

I am who survived forgive me
I am who survived forgive me
I am who survived forgive me

I am who survived don't forgive me
I am who survived don't forgive me
I am who survived don't forgive me

I am who survived hate me
I am who survived hate me
I am who survived fucking hate me kill me

I am who
I am who
I am who

I am who … helped dirt and dust and death
I am who … drove through dirt and dust and flesh and guts
I am who … kill me

I am who … Kill me not them or you or fucking kid on road
  on death on lust and blood
Dirt blood road blood
Horizon …

I am
I am
I am guilt and guts and hate and lost

I am nothing
I am lost and tired and nothing
I am lost guts throw up shit

I am who survived kill me
I am who survived
I … I I I I I I I I I I I I I I I I I I I I I I I I I I I I I I I I fuck I

I am who survived

...Aaron Hughes

THROUGH TIME OUR STORIES
WILL BE FORGOTTEN OR DISCREDITED
SO IT'S IMPORTANT TO
HAVE IT DOWN ON PAPER.

Nathan Lewis

WE'RE TRYING TO COME BACK
TO OUR LIVES.

Eli Wright

SCREAM BECAUSE YOU WANT TO

Just letting it out
the feeling inside that screams so fucking loud that your skin jumps
the feeling of not knowing a damn thing in a world of information
the feeling of insecurity of your own self
jumping off the cliffs of reality just to feel high for a while
but landing so hard that you're worse off than when you started
all I can do is jam out to great music and beat my body to
    a haunting tempo that in reality means something completely
    different than how I take it
but I don't care
this is my little spell on earth and I am going to do what
    I want with it
my time is mine, it can't be sold, bought or borrowed
but I waste so much of it on things that have already sold me out

fear is not anything it is just a lack of information
because seriously, we know what the problem is and how to
    deal with it
we cannot be affected
but we choose to live in darkness
I wish I could just think these happy thoughts but it is just
    too fucking real and too fucked
I know bigger words but I fucking choose to say fuck and for
    whatever reason it makes me feel good

depression is a curtain that covers your light
depression is a darkness that is not dull but black
so fucking dark that it changes the structure of your eye and
    you can't even look at the world the way you used to because
    your eyes are not your own
they are in the dark

pain
pain is what fear and depression feed, pain is like obesity
   to over-indulgence of depression
pain doesn't hurt, I let pain in and that hurts

It is like I am trapped in a world that no one else sees
I cannot fathom how someone can look at a child and not smile
they are the future but people make the same history-proven mistakes
we work our souls into the earth for a dollar to recreate
   a philosophy that materials mean something
when the fact is all you need is love
success is not measured by the clothes you wear, the car you drive,
   or the house you reside in
all this can be taken away. stolen, burned, or replaced

Love
LOVE
LOVE
now this is a word that is unjustified by being a word
the English say love to their children and it's also used as
   a description of how you feel
what an arrogant concept
you don't feel love
love feels you
we are not worthy to love because we are jealous, hateful,
   and vengeful beings
If love enters us, we should drop and be thankful
to experience love is what separates us from everything else
people use words like honor and devotion
what fucking bullshit
Love knows nothing else
love is love

Love is the complete opposite of hate
what a mind trip
hate consumes us all, hate is evil, hate is wrong
and love is the hand-crafted-from-God combatant of hate
and we still are so helpless to profess our love like we can
   even understand it

Love is great, I cannot articulate what love is
and I don't know how to tell people that I love them because
   I love with so much conviction

and to be completely fearless, and completely honest, I more than
love my child

stop focusing on the loss and remember what you have
life is just life so live it

...Greg Strehl

BEING BORN

Flying into Iraq on my twentieth birthday ... which happens to be Christmas Eve ... my first one away from home, and it feels like I've never been home. Never experienced what it was like to wake up and hear my Mom packing a school lunch, or riding to school with my Dad in the morning. Hard to remember skipping seventh period study hall to go meet up with friends at the coffee shop, or sneaking out during lunch with Ashley to smoke cigarettes. Peering through a mist in my mind while riding in a C-130 into a war zone, I dimly recall JROTC[1] in high school, sleepovers, fights ...

Going with Eric to the Christmas Dance my freshman year. Losing him to another girl a year later. Every girl I knew was hooked on a guy named Tim ... Tim is in Iraq too, as a Marine in Ramadi.

It's hard not to cry at times like these. I'm not scared, not of Iraq, not of car bombs, not of mortars, not of friends dying ... not yet. I'm sad. Flying into Iraq on Christmas Eve is the most alone I've ever felt in my life, and it only gets worse from here on out. There's no snow, there's no trees, there's no Santa ... and there's no Mom and Dad, no friends, no family. I miss the awkward family gatherings where an uncle gets too drunk and some aunt or cousin says something inappropriate or someone gets stiffed on a present.

Sneaking a drink with Allie three years too young. Hiding a case of Coors Light from my parents ... in my dresser. Everything seems like it never happened. It's as if I'm twenty years old and I never existed before.

As it turns out, that's how the whole year felt.

Now, two years later, I try to enjoy myself at a street fair, and all I can think about is how in Iraq, if the streets were this crowded, a car would explode and there'd be body parts strewn everywhere. It's hard not to cry during times like these. Twenty-two years old, married, and just learning how to exist.

...Sarah Wallace

---

[1] Junior Reserve Officer Training Corps

ON DEATH—FREQUENT THOUGHTS

Time please grant me solace, in this slender life I mime
Life's a tendon strung taut, another senseless rhyme
On what note will that string snap back, and reverberate my dying
How will the song be played out, and sung while earthworms dine
So lower my body down down, into the sweet chill ground
I've thought in life and of death, but which is more profound
Can you feel life flowing, as if through open wounds?
Like a cold wind blowing slowly, throughout your dying rooms
Like staring sharply forward, while life and death commune
Or sleeping through the morning, and wasting afternoons
So plant my broken body, into the sweet chill ground
Will I still feel your sorrow, when my corpse is six feet down?
Sing for me a new song, to represent the years
That's what my life should sound like, to family, friends and peers
A strange new hymn that's sadly, familiar to your ears
One that I hope reminds you, of a laugh, or curse, or tears
So lay my cold frail body, into the sweet chill ground
And bring a rose or trinket, next time you come around
In death harsh winds and hatred, are well beyond your reach
There are no more wretched lessons, for love and life to teach
Not one more selfish sermon, for the frightened ones to preach
To tell you that some heaven, is a darker grey for each
So don't lay me down down, into that sweet chill ground
Till I've bled the very last drop, from every friend around
Life is not but memories that no amount could buy
Times that make you want to, laugh or curse or cry
When my life is flashing, before my very eyes
I want that it should take a lifetime passing by.

...Toby Hartbarger

RUNNING
JOURNAL ENTRY, APRIL 22, 2003 7:47 PM

I find myself running and hiding all the time. Running and hiding from life, from the pain and agony it brings. It builds up inside of me, I feel the fire, it's burning my thoughts, my head, it blinds me, my thoughts my dreams all gone to waste.

Just letting reality melt away. Now fear starts to kick in but I like it. I am familiar with not knowing what to expect next. Whether it be a fit of rage or blinding desire to destroy everything around me. I go blank. I know not what I do, I see not what I've done, it's all a blur. Emotions what are those? I can't tell anymore. Is this a dream or more like a nightmare when will it end? When will the pain I suffer go away? **Go into someone else's mind?**

Mine is all chewed up. I run and run just to find out what I am running from, it is me that I am running from. I'm a demon in my own life. I'm that darkness that falls on my own day, eating at my own thoughts. Destroying my own core. I'm too far for you to reach your hand out to help me because I've already given up. I am not what I show you nor what you think. I am something else.

When you close your eyes you will see me, when you walk alone I am behind you, when you hear a whisper, you have heard me but I know you will not find me. What makes you think you can look for me if you know not what I am? I hear voices in my head, I hear laughter at me, I know I have failed in life and I am a tool that has been molded and slowly spiraling day by day until I am sucked in that darker place of no return only to suffer more.

I ask, is there a God, if so, why so much pain, why? I tried to kill the pain, but only brought more, much more. I'm pouring crimson regret, and betrayal I'm dying, praying bleeding screaming, am too lost to be saved. Where is my tourniquet?

My pain cries for the grave, I want to suffer no more. I am nothing I will be nothing. No one understands. I have given all of myself to others only to find they betray me. I've lost myself a long time ago or maybe I never was. All I see is death. There is no life, no hope. There is no meaning to life but to suffer. I have realized that my own children are now being brought into this suffering and I am sorry I have done this to them, it is my fault.

What is being happy? Is there such a thing, or is it all false? Is there realization of what life is to be? What is the meaning of life? Well I tell you, it is fixed in a manner for failure and misery. I do not want anything anymore only to have it cause more pain.

You're a twisted little fuck Leonard, and you always have been. You weak little shit, fucking cry-baby, you're not a man, you can't be one, nor will you ever amount to anything. I have proven this to you already and you know it, how many times do I have to show your stupid ass?

The end of the ride is coming, murder, suicide, is how I've been feeling. I have let you see death and you know it is coming, I have shown it to you in many ways and I know what it has done to you. Cpl Cotto died and the other 7 Marines. You looked at it first hand and I gave it to you. I let you see it, I wanted you to see it. And you have been living it everyday of your life since. And you think you can stop it from coming to you, OK, watch. We are almost there boy.

I want these voices in my head to stop. I hear them too clearly and loudly. I can't cut them off, I can't stop seeing the horrible things I have seen first hand, I can't get out of my mind things I have done to hide the pain I feel. I am so tired of lies about life, lies I have told, I am tired. The heat is coming, again I feel it. It is burning inside of me, my head hurts, it burns, it burns, I feel like I am on fire inside. I have been running for years and there is nowhere else to run, I am tired, so tired.

...Leonard Shelton

PTSD

Post-Traumatic Stress Disorder.

How is this a *disorder*?

What part of being emotionally and spiritually affected
by gross violence is *disorder*?

How about a *going to war and coming home with
a clear conscience* disorder?

I think that would be far more appropriate.

...Matt Howard

AND THEN I SAW IT

And then I saw it.
Who is this boy who sits in the tree?
Cries for you. Cries for me.
Take back your wish, you wished too hard.
In your blindness you stumbled
And found the right moment and now,
Now just look what you have done—
Now look what you have done.
She angrily clucks
And the blade floats there.
It's coming for you too.
Take back your wish!
I can't feel my legs because I have no legs you stupid whore!
Insatiable fat and greasy gourd, wanting more.
Take that spike from the sky and throw it into the ocean.
It has all been a lie
And you run and you go and you do
And there is nowhere to run to.
I tried to tell you so—
I tried to tell you so.

Who is this boy who sits without a hand?
You should have never left the tree
And I tried to tell you so
Stop touching tender tears
They are not for you
They are for me!
Don't comfort me
I don't want you flag disease.
Don't cry to me with humble eyes and outstretched blood—
If I cannot hear, how can I sing?
I am broken.
I am numb.

Pain is no pain in the song unsung.
Take, eat, this is my body.
I don't want it any more
And I tried to tell you.
I tried to tell you.
Now will you listen, now that it's too late?
Breathe deep the toxic fumes of my annihilation
And I will take you with me.
I do not speak your language
Or care to understand.
I will stand and scream my own and fuck your eyes.
Beat, beat, beat. There is nothing left to build.
Stop, I say, it is too late.
Sing your pretty song and dance stars on me
I do not want your help.
The black bleating heart sends waves of disgust from my
From your
To my
And I cannot hear. I will not hear.
And how many days did you expect that I should stand there waiting?
Save your own fucking life
And take your hands blood off me I am not dead.
I am not dead.
I see you there laughing on the battlefield playground.
Where will the children go now that you have blacked them?
Who will want to eat where you have shat?
Who will cry for mother when all who loved her have gone?
Who will give bread to mother
Now that her brave oven holds devil's child?
How will you learn and marry and grow
And continue your ridiculous planning now that you hang there?
Who will take my deeper thoughts and turn them to laughter
Now that you are gone?
The hands box is empty and you dare to come to me for mine?
I have no hands, or heart, or ears—

You have taken them with you
And all of me is gone.
How could you take the faggot child
Into your dark world of angry toys?
And how could you take his pretty light and grind it into the sand?
And how could you lead him by trusting hand and portend to teach
When you are the rightful pupil?
Now look what you have done!
Stop eyes saying
There is nothing to say.
Go or don't go
It doesn't matter anyway.
Cold creeping hands in foreign lands.
Stay home! Stay home! Stay home!
You can't call yourself a name
When the father is dead.
The father is dead and has taken his name!
His name and his potential
His better hope and rising.
You will die too and those after you.
I have killed us all.
I have been risen and I chose death.
Why come to me with blame and hunger?
I cannot feed you with empty bowl.
Young and stupid to trust me child.
It was a lie and I was pretending—
Scared and a child myself
I cannot grow from fear.
Go home and ask your mother
She is not there.
My brother fucked her and turned her to air.
Bush good! Bush good!
I take my blade.
Bush good! Bush good!
I place it there.
Bush good! Bush good!

And I push it in and save you from a life in Hell.

My hate of my king
And love of him too,
To hate your king
And I kill too
And enough and more 'til the killin's done.
And look at the bad guy
He's on the run
And he's runnin' to Hell to bring back some more
And you'll taste my rage and there's oh, so much more—
And I'll kill myself too
But not before you.

The sun has gone to chase the moon
And left us all in this cold empty room
Of no playgrounds or forests or deserts prestine.
The Ferris wheel's been painted dull marine green.

And now I must leave you and run to the crowds
They're cheering and beating
Their palm's blood and loud—
And they're crying and laughing
And taste sweet relief
From their debt and their anguish and their bed-wetting grief
And they blow me and hold me and call me their king
But the joke is on them, no hand means no ring
And no head means no crown
And my shame smile from their loving
Washed permanent frown.

Empty chains lonely, they all deserve tags
So we'll fill all the coffers, turn raiment to rags
And we'll drink all the oil
And hide all the gold
And we'll make you all niggers
You'll serve 'til you're old
And your children will leave you

And carry no pain
When they learn to dance in our poisonous rain.
Hear how they tinkle when the wind makes them sway.
September eleventh is just another day
And nothing makes sense when it all becomes clear
A minute's a month and a month is a year
And all
Will
Soon
Be
Forgotten.
What? You thought I would remember you?
I don't even know myself.
Someone take her away from me
Her filthy hands may soil my beautiful dress.

The boy has fallen from the tree.
The salt taste ants have gone
And the needle nose sucker too.
One Iraq fly, now gone too.
Gone.
And there is nothing.

...Jeff Key

ROAD TO BAGHDAD – GARETT REPPENHAGEN

THE WALKING DEAD

My life has changed; at times I feel I never knew who I was.
Your lifeless bodies laying on the desert floor, and we were told to
keep going. I was frozen, and something inside of me left my body.
I couldn't go on. Your life was taken in front of me—how could
I leave you like that? I had to continue the fight. I left you brothers.
I'm sorry I had to go fight. Where do I go? How do I fix it? I'm still
afraid, wondering where to help and find you. I want to take care
of you; you should be lying there lifeless on the desert floor. How
is your family going to know? Will they be told the truth? Where
are you? I'm trying to find you. Your lives were taken by greedy
men who never took the time to know who you are. I live my life
to honor the dead—which in turn I do not live, because if I leave
I betray them. I am not alive; I am the walking dead. I like to know
or just have a day to know the better side of life, and what it would
be like. Death, murder, confusion, lost soul, the ghost has left my
body and it does not know how to get back in. I search every day
trying to find it, but where is it? It's gone, teasing, never to return.
We talked about coming home. Cpl. Cotto, where are you. I am
lost, but you and the others are gone.

I now live my life pretending everything is okay with a smile on my
face, but every day I am empty. Take a good look in my eyes and tell
me what you see.

...Leonard Shelton

WHO SURVIVED?

forgive me
because
I am
who survived

...Evan Moodie

AMBULANCE – KELLY DOUGHERTY

COMING HOME

driving in my newly purchased vehicle
somewhere in Pennsylvania
there's a semitruck ahead of me
trying to make it up the hill
he has to downshift and the power is sent to the wheels

I notice the exhaust pipes
above the cab of his truck
a large puff of black smoke
fills the air
I thought I was back
in the mess I had come from
another explosion and my heart skips a beat

Back in Vermont, it's so nice to be home
the smells are finally sweet again
and there's no more aircraft
hounding the skies

But back with my family
so happy to see me
they always would ask
"so, then, how was it?"

It's hard to reply
when they haven't seen it
"nothing much happened"
is all I could say

...Evan Moodie

WHOSE SOUL IS THAT?

I have a huge gaping hole in my soul

My body has all of its extremities

Ten fingers and ten toes just like the day I was born

But now, I have a huge gaping hole in my soul

You can only see it through the violent shaking of my
hands and the excessive bouncing of my knees and the
uneasiness of the breaths I can barely take

You can only hear it when the constant vomiting and
shitting leaks through the bathroom door

I feel the sand on my face, awakening, as if a black
hawk just took off the flight line

No, it's just the rumble of a truck passing my parents'
house

Where did all this weakness and fear come from?

The gaping hole drips with pain
Ragged are the edges where they ripped her heart out
Emptiness is all you find where her loving soul used to be
Anger and hatred is now her contagious disease

Don't ever look into her eyes

...Jennifer Pacanowski

BURDENED AND BATTERED AND BURIED ALIVE*

I've never felt so alone as I did in December 2005. I had been honorably discharged from the Marine Corps in July 2005. I missed my buddies. Other veterans wouldn't get scared when they saw me staring off, unconsciously, into the desert in my mind. I knew my family loved me, but the son my mother raised never came home from Fallujah. Anyway, back to December. I had tried to go to the VA in Los Angeles, but got the runaround, so I left for Missouri to find some real help. I got there in December. I spent every night in December with a loaded shotgun by my side in case I needed to end the pain, end the burden; I was battered emotionally, and the VA, along with my country, had buried me alive.

...Cloy Richards

---

* Title comes from a line in the poem entitled "Dirt" by Garett Reppenhagen

GHOST LIMB

my open palm searched for the missing guard
and in my weariness attempted to curl around it
the other hand dreamed of the grip it once supported
my cheek yearned for the stock it rested upon
my nose reached for the charging handle
that once set my consistent sight picture
my eyes scan for the front sight post
invisible now before my target
all the while my finger readies to kill again
oh the comfortable caress of my cradle rifle
some amputees say they can still feel their missing limbs

...Garett Reppenhagen

UNTITLED — LOVELLA CALICA

UNTITLED — LOVELLA CALICA

JUNKIES

Young hands dispense drinking equipment

Feeding the relentless machine

Coffee is the drug

The weathered waitress is the pusher

And I … I am the junkie

We are all junkies

Prozac, weed, Viagra, heroin

Television, computers, cars, oil, electricity, convenience …

If religion is the opiate of the masses

Does that explain why crazy zealots ruined this country

They must have been high

And what of those who worship science, technology,
  and the almighty dollar?

What happens to their eternal spirit?

It seems that my every thought is a question

Feel something!

Even anger is better than apathy and cynicism

...Mike Blake

WAR

revolution starts with saying no
no more of this
no listening to lies
pretending not to hear cries
I signed to protect the innocent
not to kill them
all this rage pent up in my cage
like a rabid evil letting loose
watch my fist start flying like a snowstorm on you
my war is with you
I am here for the tens of thousands of lives
I am here for the widowed wives
I am here to catch mother's cries
I am here to expose the lies
What about the children without their dad?
Fuck yeah I am mad
Mr. President with your arrogant smile

...Greg Strehl

SURELY THE WAY

Surely the way has long been lost
for what noble cause did we withstand the tempestuous tide
did we serve and sacrifice ...

And even to this day we are sent to pay for crooked gains
putting out the flames we didn't create
and taking the brunt of stirred-up hate ...

Surely an integral part of ourselves has been laid to waste
and who knows how long rebuilding it will take
in the end of human errors, everyone has their own soul at stake
As long as there is breath and life, there is always time to
  make it right ...

yet you will never be able to regain what was lost
in the way of human life
in the way of hope
in the way of faith
while you take your time in correcting the mistakes
which raise their voices louder and louder
every day

...Raymond Camper

SINGLE VOICE

my single voice echoes in the hallways of reality
kissing your life goodbye and saying hello to hell with a smile
  and determination is a wonderful thing
when I speak like this I know that you understand
you may not want to admit it or you may even think you just
  like the sounds of the words
but you have to feel me
inside outside looking between
why can't there be a world without any sides
or be by my side?
are we all just aliens? Why do we pretend not to see what's
  right in front of us?
why when something becomes clear that everyone else knew
  seem like the shock was out of this world?
home?
home is not where you lay your head
home is not where your heart lies
my heart is not in my house
home is what they cannot take from you
I know what home is and my head has nothing to do with it
so many tears fall with no one to catch them
moonlight shining in my eyes and I am enchanted by
  just seeing the stars
to lose yourself but still hold on to what you are
heroes are not born or made or even tangible
what makes a hero?
someone to help?
stop evil?
protect the innocent?
what the fuck man isn't that life??????

I really don't know what I am trying to say
but I know what I am talking about
you know when the pressure of silence
combust into flames
there is no shame
you owe it to yourself to let it loose
everything was let loose on you
Am I in your head yet or does this just seem like gibberish?
How great would it be to pretend to have Tourette's syndrome
and just yell out what you really think any time you felt it?
why do we hold it all in?
this is my voice
hear my whisper
the gentle pitch that makes ears bleed
this is my voice
this is me
forget the poetic shit
I feel so dead, alive, sad, happy, and confused about it all
Some prisons don't have bars
But I know that it will shine again
the green of my eyes will turn a baby white
and words of happiness will run from my fingers
   like Olympic athletes
faith is a wonderful thing
people have lived for faith
some have died for faith
and all faith is a belief that your hope will come true
the world is such a large place and people are so closed off
How can we let our brothers and sisters die over rich man's
   greed and watch TV?
what the fuck does that do to me?
hate just breeds

we are taught politics in school but not how to love
control is all around you but lack of control is you
by not choosing anything you have made the biggest
   choice of wrong
how dare we have this beautiful mind that no one or
   no machine can understand?
how dare any of us let someone else make up our own mind?
my single voice has tired my body
but I know I have to keep going on
I don't have any more to say for now but my single voice
   will never stop.

...Greg Strehl

COMING HOME

A Boeing 777

A long flight home
I asked a stewardess to sit on me
She looked at me like I had just gotten out of Iraq
Sand still stuck in my ears and my hair
You can never wash it all out
I sat next to other NCOs[1] and planned my first meal stateside
We landed

A white bus
We drove almost three hours from March Air Field to Las Pulgas
in Camp Pendleton. As we pulled onto the parade deck, involuntary
specters wearing foreign looking green cammies stood in formation
to greet us home

My family was the only civilians there to welcome the troops home
No tickertape
No scantily clad cheerleaders
No rivers of beer
Just a cheating fiancée
An empty bank account
And a brokendown Chevy truck

...Cloy Richards

---

[1] Non-Commissioned Officers

COMING HOME

I bought a car. A '68 Mustang… where do I go? Where do I go?
Who do I talk to? I don't know who I should be, talk to, be with,
sleep with. I can't sit at home. I can't be alone. Family at work,
friends at school, life was gone a year ago. Who do I talk to?
Drive … alone
I'll drive anywhere, go anywhere
Just show me, tell me where I belong
Drive … dark, lights, radio loud louder
I'm lost.
Where do I go, who do I talk to?
Pull over high school. My high school four five years gone. My high
school with the phone by the gym that I would call for rides home.
I would wait at these doors for my mother to come. High school
dark alone car engine on. Humming.

Hello
Brian
Hey man, where you at?
Should I come over there?
I know it's … I know it's late.
Can I come over there?
Soon?
Dude, I don't know where to go … who to call.
I haven't seen you.
I can drive there.
Two hours … Three hours … We can see each other.
Soon?
Yeah soon.
Car drive Chicago alone drive
I haven't been alone in so long. I don't want to be alone. Don't
close the door when I sleep. I need to hear you in the other room.
Who do I call? Where do I go. Drive.

Hello.
Del.
Can I see you?
No?
No. I know I can't just call you but I don't know who to call
where to go.
Drive. Drive. Drive streetlights fall Chicago air I am alone and the
clubs are closed. Where do I go? Who do I call? Drive. Drive.
Tell the truth.

...Aaron Hughes

WHO SURVIVED?

they tell me not to have any guilt
but how can that be
when I would like to see
the reason for their deaths

Forgive me, please
Forgive them, too
I am one of many
who survived this
I am surviving every day
from the guilt
of having been there

...Evan Moodie

LIBERATE

Information distortion through paradigms of power
Justify aggression, turn the propaganda louder
History sanitized by the state
Fear an emotion to manipulate
Freedom of speech under watchful eye
Freedom of speech, just don't ask why
'Cause they've got the will to kill, to eat and drink
their fill
For their fill they've got the will to kill, to see
our blood spill

Is the lust for more worth the price of war?
Is the lust for more worth fighting for?

...Thomas Buonomo

CONVOY OPS

We took their oath
They signed our sentence
Now we're lined up on the border
Like sheep being led to our slaughter

The thump of the mortars
and tracers in the sky
Welcome to Iraq
It's the 4th of July

Everything we touch with our weapons of mass distraction
Covered in poison dust, destroyed beyond recognition
The sands are shifting and the rivers are running dry
The children are thirsty but too dehydrated to cry

A year at war
A lifetime defined
History is written
But time passes us by

I wish I wasn't a veteran
Stuck in the past
They tell me to move on
But the memories last

I just want to sleep again
Feel like a human again
Returning to a home that will never be home again
I never thought I'd write another poem again

...Eli Wright

BROKEN TOY SOLDIERS

We buy broken hearts, and boil them in white pots
We mix 'em up, cook 'em up, and feed them to our dogs
And when the dogs have had their fill, and say they've had enough
We wait until they shit 'em up, and gather up the stuff

We put the hearts in buckets, and give 'em to the chefs
Who roll them out on baking sheets, and stick on top the chips
Then they throw them in the oven, and cook them till they're well
Then we feed them to the kiddies, who say "Gee sir, they're swell!"

Then we hand the kids a little flag, which they begin to wave
Stick 'em in the audience of a Veteran's Day Parade
As the troops go marching by, with flashbacks in their eyes
They see the bright-eyed angels, and they begin to sigh

For once a long, long time ago, they stood on the side
Till a recruiter came to them and told them all his lies
Then they're standing in an office, standing proud and tall
They look all around 'em, see a hundred others in the hall

They hold up their right hands, they say they'll do it all
Then we send them off to war, where they see all around them fall
Kids, soldiers, dreams, hopes
Till all that stand are broken toy soldiers

Yes we buy broken hearts of now-childless moms
And sell them in ribbons in booths at strip malls
We buy broken hearts of now-widowed wives
Who work hard everyday to keep their kids alive
We buy broken hearts of now-broken men
Then make them reenlist, for heartless men will do it again
We buy broken hearts of now-fatherless sons
Wait till they grow up, and sell them all our guns
Send them off to fight in a different-but-same war
Tell them "Hajji killed your dad," so they'll kill more and more

Yes, we buy broken hearts and stick 'em in our songs
We buy broken hearts and insert 'em in our speeches
We buy broken hearts and stick 'em on the back of
  our pickup trucks
We buy broken hearts to help our war machine go round
And soon one day we'll buy yours, and throw you in the ground

...Mark Wilkerson

RECALL A VETERAN: TO GO BACK TO WAR

I'm no longer your robot
I don't do what I'm told
I don't play the game
I don't believe what you say
I don't do it this way

I'm not your machine
I won't do as I'm told
I won't play that game
I won't believe what you say
I won't do it that way
I'm not a number

I can't follow those rules
I can't wear those boots
I can't use that gun
I can't speak as you do

So then:
I'm not going
I won't be your slave
I don't need the stress
I can't deal with that mess

In other words, please:
Just leave me alone
Stop sending me shit
And calling my phone

...Evan Moodie

RED ROCKS — LOVELLA CALICA

LETTER TO MY FUTURE SELF

Dear Aaron,

I hope that you are at peace right now. I hope that you have found a space to be. I'm not sure I should remind you of something that I hope you have not forgotten. Remember Ahmed and NYC? That was it, you know, a time of life where for once you felt and understood love ... love and compassion. I hope you are not frustrated. Remember life and compassion and eternity and death are all sad but beautiful. I hope you've stopped the fucking war.

Damn, what a thought, the war still dragging on for nothing but nothing. Damn, wars should end and be over and in peace. But, fuck Aaron it's only been ten years and I hope you have not forgotten it will take a lifetime to rebuild Iraq. If you have not gone back to that dust and gray sand ... Go.

Get off your ass. Drop whatever self-righteous thing you believe you are doing and go to Iraq and help.

Help build a house, paint a mural, start an art space. Get to know and understand Iraq and Iraqis. Get to know everything the military did not tell you.

Aaron, go.

And don't forget "a bird knows no barbed wire."

Sincerely,
Younger you

...Aaron Hughes

A WORD IS WORTH A THOUSAND PICTURES

6 Marines
3 standing tall and proud in the foreground
3 crouching in the background
6 Marines posing in Fallujah, supposedly the
  "Graveyard of Americans"
6 young, strong men with battle-hardened countenances
6 marines in great health posing with rifles, deep in enemy territory
How brave they look, how American
They can go to any country in the world, kick ass and take
  pictures to show the folks back home what their tax dollars are
  paying for.
That picture of my buddies and I is forever in my mind,
  yet slightly changed

Private Perez was killed by a car bomber at a vehicle checkpoint.
There's only 5 Marines in the picture now.

Sergeant Silva lost the use of his left leg after a rocket attack
  and now is addicted to painkillers and booze.
There's only 4 Marines in the picture now.

Lance Corporal Dubois joined the Marines to help conquer his
heroin addiction. After three years clean and sober, he came home
from Iraq a broken man, and turned back to heroin. He overdosed
two months after we got back
There's only 3 Marines in the picture now.

Corporal Allen's stress and emotional problems got the better of
him and he started beating his wife and children. Two years after
Iraq he's in prison, without a family.
There's only 2 Marines in the picture now.

Private First Class Anderson got dishonorably discharged for
drug use 5 months after we came home. Rather than turn to his
family for help, he wanders the streets of southern California,
begging for money, food, work.

There's 1 Marine left in the picture now, and it's me.
Am I still alive?
I might be physically breathing, but I'm dying inside.

So really there aren't any Marines in that picture and without those
Marines it's just a picture of a shattered city in a devastated country.

...Cloy Richards

LETTER TO MYSELF TEN YEARS FROM NOW

Dear you, me, us, whatever,

How's that war in Iraq going? Are we still fighting them over
there so we don't have to fight them over here? You know we still
want to walk the Appalachian Trail and see Europe, so we better
have taken care of that. Are we still having nightmares? Are we
still drinking and smoking? Have we had a son yet? Are we going
to tell him about what happened in Fallujah? I hope we're still
trying … trying to be normal, trying to sleep without drugs, trying
to find a justification for our existence. I know God didn't put us
here to kill those people. Don't forget about them. If you haven't
already … forgive yourself for that, just don't forget it. Oh yeah,
are the fucking Cubs ever going to win another World Series?
Hit me back.

Peace,
you

…Cloy Richards

CONTRIBUTORS

Paul Abernathy
Pittsburgh, PA
Baghdad/Al Anbar/Balad, Iraq: March 2003–2004
Army Reserves: 1996–2004
459 En Co., 1st Marine Expeditionary Force, 3rd ID, and V Corps
12C Combat Engineer (bridge crewmember)

Phil Aliff
Atlanta, GA
Abu Ghraib, Iraq: August 2005–July 2006
US Army: November 2004–current
10th Mountain Division
11B Infantryman

Luke Austin
Rochester, MN
IL ARNG: January 2004–January 2010
139th Mobile Public Affairs Detachment
46Q photojournalist

Michael Blake
Syracuse, NY
Iraq: April 2003–March 2004
US Army: 2001–2005
4th Infantry Division, 92Y Supply Specialist
Upon return from Iraq, he filed for Conscientious Objector status
and received an Honorable Discharge.

Fernando Braga
Bronx, NY
Camp Cedar II, Iraq: March 2004–January 2005
ARNG: September 2001–September 2007
369 Corps Support Battalion
92Y Supply Specialist

Maria Braga is a 24 year old ESL Learning Specialist at East Bronx
Academy for the Future. She teases her husband, Fernando Braga,
about the fact that she sees more blood teaching in the Bronx than
he did in Iraq.

Thomas J. Buonomo
Rochester, NY
US Army: 2002–2007
C 304th MI BN
35D Military Intelligence
He was discharged for voicing his political views before
his deployment date.

Drew Cameron
Burlington, VT
Iraq: April 2003–December 2003
US Army: August 2000–2006
Bravo Battery 6th Battalion 27th Field Artillery Regiment
13M MLRS Crewmember

Raymond Camper
Mahtomedi, MN
Fallujah/Al Taqaddum, Iraq: April 2006–July 2007
MN ARNG: 2003–2009
E Co. 134th FSC,
Chaplains Assistant, Admin Spec.

Bryan Casler
Rochester, NY
Iraq: March 2003–May 2003
Afghanistan: September 2004–February 2005
Iraq: September 2005–March 2006
USMC: 2002–2006
2nd Battalion 6th Marines Fox Company
0311 Rifleman

Justin C. Cliburn
Lawton, OK
Baghdad, Iraq: December 2005–December 2006
OK ARNG: 2001–current
1st Bn 158th FA
13M MLRS crewmember, served as an MP

Kelly Dougherty
Philadelphia, PA
Iraq/Kuwait: February 2003–February 2004
CO ARNG: 1996–2004
220th MP Company
HQ Detachment 5, Medical unit
91B Medic 95B Military Police

Vincent J.R. Emanuele
Chesterton, IN
Al Qaim/Al Asad/Kuwait, Iraq: August 2004–April 2005
USMC: September 2002–January 2006
1st Battalion 7th Marines Alpha Co. 3rd Platoon
Rifleman

Eric Estenzo
Los Angeles, CA
Basrah province, Babil province, Iraq: March 2002–September 2002
USMC: 1999–2005
H&S Co. 4th LAR Battalion 4th MAR DIV
2147 Light Armored Vehicle Technician

Toby Hartbarger
Philadelphia, PA
Baghdad/Fallujah/Najaf/Al Kut, Iraq: April 2003–July 2004
US Army: 2002–2004
Apache Troop 1/2 ACR
11C Infantry Mortarman

Clifton Hicks
Gainesville, FL
Baghdad, Iraq: October 2003–July 2004
US Army: May 2003–December 2005
C Troop 1st Squadron 1st Cavalry Regiment
19K M1 Abrams Crewman (tanker)

Jen Hogg
New York, NY
NY ARNG: 2000–2005
152 Engr Bn, 42 ID
63Y Truck Mechanic

Jared Hood
Denver, CO
US Army Reserves/CO ARNG: 2003–2007
One year was spent serving on active duty
5025th MP detachment and the 220th MP
31B MP

Matt Howard
Burlington, VT
Kuwait/Iraq: January 2003–August 2003
Kuwait: April 2004–July 2004
USMC: November 2001–November 2005
1st Tank Bn
7 ton operator

Matt Hrutkay
New York City, NY
Abu Ghraib, Iraq: August 2005–August 2006
US Army: 2003–2006
A Co., 2-22 INF, 1st BCT, 10th Mtn Div.
11B infantryman

Aaron Hughes
Chicago, IL
Camp Arifjan, Iraq/Kuwait: April 2003–July 2004
IL ARNG: 2000–2006
1244th Transportation Co.
88M Transporter

Dave Kalbfleish
Arlington Heights, IL
Arabian Gulf: March 2003–October 2003
US Navy: 2001–2006
USS Pasadena
Submarine Officer, unrestricted line

Sholom Keller
Philadelphia, PA
Kandahar, Afghanistan: January 2002–July 2002
Iraq: March 2003–February 2004
US Army: 2001–2005
101st Airborne Division
Commo

Jeff Key
Salt Lake City, UT
Eastern Iraq: April 2003–June 2003
USMC: 2000–2006
4th LAR Bat.
2147-LAV technician (driver for the R variant during deployment)

Evan Michael Knappenberger
Bellingham, WA
Taji, Iraq: December 2005–December 2006
US Army: 2003–2007
A. Co. 1st STB, 4th Infantry
96B Intelligence Analyst

Nathan Lewis
Barker, NY
Iraq: March 2003–July 2003
U.S Army: 2001–2003
1st 14th Artillery Battalion
13M-MLRS Crewmember

Evan R. Moodie
Walla Walla, WA
Al Asad Air Base, Iraq: September 2004–March 2005
USMC: 2002–2006
2nd Battalion 10th Marines 2nd Marine division
0844 artillery fire direction control (FDC), provisional infantry

Michael Nowacki
Chicago, IL
Baghdad, Iraq: July 2004–March 2005
US Army: July 1990–March 1992, November 1996–January 2006
D Company 110th MI Bat.
97B Counterintelligence Agent/11B Infantryman

Matthew Ornstein
Chicago, IL
Northern Arabian Gulf/Umm Qasr, Iraq: March 2003–May 2003
US Coast Guard: August 1999–August 2003
USCGC Walnut WLB205
Damage Controlman

Jennifer Pacanowski
Henryville, PA
Iraq: January 2004–December 2004
US Army: 2003–2005
557th Medical Evac
Combat Medic/Health Care Specialist

Garett Reppenhagen
Manitou Springs, CO
Baquba, Iraq: January 2004–January 2005
US Army: 2001–2005
2-63 AR BN, 1st Infantry Division
19D Cavalry Scout Sniper

Cloy Richards
Salem, MO
An Najaf/Baghdad, Iraq: March 2003–October 2003
Fallujah, Iraq: March 2004–October 2004
USMC: 2001–2005
1st Marine Division
0811 Field Artillery Cannoneer

W. Chris Ritter
Norman, OK
Camp Arifjan, Iraq/Kuwait: March 2003–September 2003
USN: 1987–2000
OK ARNG: 2000–current
B Co 2nd 149AVN 45th Brigade
15U CH-47 Flight Engineer

Eric Salazar
Seattle, WA
Persian Gulf, Kuwait/Iraq: March 2003–June 2003
USMC: 2001–2004
Heavy Marine Helicopter Squadron 465
CH-53E Helicopter Mechanic/Crew Chief

Colin Sesek
Boise, ID
Tikrit/Tal Afar, Iraq: August 2006–October 2007
US Army: 2004–2008
82nd Airborne Division
68W Medic

Leonard Shelton
Lakewood, OH
Desert Storm: August 1990–March 1991
Kosovo: July 2002–August 2002
USMC: December 1984–December 2004
Combat 1st LARBn A-Co
0311 rifleman, 0313 LAV crewman
0369 infantry unit leader, 8511 Drill Instructor

Martin Smith
Champaign, IL
USMC: 1997-2002
1st Rad BN
2791 Russian Linguist

Greg Strehl
Townsville, Queensland of Australia
Iraq: March 2003–June 2003
USMC: 2000–2004
1st Tank BN H&S Co Maint Plt
2146 MBT Technician

Jon Michael Turner
Fallujah/Abu Gharib, Iraq: January 2005–August 2005
Ramadi, Iraq: March–October 2006
USMC: August 2003–October 2007
K Co. 3rd Bn. 8th Marines
0311 Infantry, Automatic Machine Gunner

Sara Wallace
Grabill, IN
Camp Liberty, Iraq: December 2005–November 2006
US Army: 2004–2007
4ID G2 Section
96B Intel Analyst

Mark Wilkerson
Colorado Springs, CO
Tikrit, Iraq: March 2003–March 2004
US Army: June 2002–July 2007
40st Military Police Company in the 720th Military Police Battalion
31B-Military Police
When his Conscientious Objector packet was denied, he went AWOL.
Mark later turned himself in and served 5 months in a military prison.

Eli Wright
Denver, CO
Ramadi, Iraq: September 2003–September 2004
US Army: 2002–current
1st Infantry Division
Combat Medic